Rulers of the Middle Ages

By Rafael Tilton

LUCENT BOOKS

An imprint of Thomson Gale, a part of The Thomson Corporation

Detroit • New York • San Francisco • San Diego • New Haven, Conn.
Waterville, Maine • London • Munich

LIBRARY OF CONGRESS CATALOGING-IN-PUBLICATION DATA

Tilton, Rafael.
  Rulers of the Middle Ages / by Rafael Tilton.
    p. cm. -- (History makers)
  Includes bibliographical references and index.
  ISBN 1-59018-264-2 (alk. paper)
  1. Kings and rulers, Medieval—Biography. 2. Middle Ages—History. 3. Europe—
History—476-1492. I. Title. II. Series.
D115.T55 2004
940.1'092'2—dc22   2004010828

CONTENTS

2007 2096 Station 711

FOREWORD

The literary form most often referred to as "multiple biography" was perfected in the first century A.D. by Plutarch, a perceptive and talented moralist and historian who hailed from the small town of Chaeronea in central Greece. His most famous work, *Parallel Lives*, consists of a long series of biographies of noteworthy ancient Greek and Roman statesmen and military leaders. Frequently, Plutarch compares a famous Greek to a famous Roman, pointing out similarities in personality and achievements. These expertly constructed and very readable tracts provided later historians and others, including playwrights like Shakespeare, with priceless information about prominent ancient personages and also inspired new generations of writers to tackle the multiple biography genre.

The Lucent History Makers series proudly carries on the venerable tradition handed down from Plutarch. Each volume in the series consists of a set of five to eight biographies of important and influential historical figures who were linked together by a common factor. In *Rulers of Ancient Rome*, for example, all the figures were generals, consuls, or emperors of either the Roman Republic or Empire; while the subjects of *Fighters Against American Slavery*, though they lived in different places and times, all shared the same goal, namely the eradication of human servitude. Mindful that politicians and military leaders are not (and never have been) the only people who shape the course of history, the editors of the series have also included representatives from a wide range of endeavors, including scientists, artists, writers, philosophers, religious leaders, and sports figures.

Each book is intended to give a range of figures—some well known, others less known; some who made a great impact on history, others who made only a small impact. For instance, by making Columbus's initial voyage possible, Spain's Queen Isabella I, featured in *Women Leaders of Nations*, helped to open up the New World to exploration and exploitation by the European powers. Unarguably, therefore, she made a major contribution to a series of events that had momentous consequences for the entire world. By contrast, Catherine II, the eighteenth-century Russian queen, and Golda Meir, the modern Israeli prime minister, did not play roles of global impact; however, their policies and actions significantly influenced the historical development of both their own countries and their regional neighbors. Regardless of their relative importance in the greater historical scheme, all of the figures chronicled in the History Makers series made contributions to posterity; and their public achievements, as well as what is known about their private lives, are presented and evaluated in light of the most recent scholarship.

In addition, each volume in the series is documented and substantiated by a wide array of primary and secondary source quotations. The primary source quotes enliven the text by presenting eyewitness views of the times and culture in which each history maker lived; while the secondary source quotes, taken from the works of respected modern scholars, offer expert elaboration and/ or critical commentary. Each quote is footnoted, demonstrating to the reader exactly where biographers find their information. The footnotes also provide the reader with the means of conducting additional research. Finally, to further guide and illuminate readers, each volume in the series features photographs, two bibliographies, and a comprehensive index.

The History Makers series provides both students engaged in research and more casual readers with informative, enlightening, and entertaining overviews of individuals from a variety of circumstances, professions, and backgrounds. No doubt all of them, whether loved or hated, benevolent or cruel, constructive or destructive, will remain endlessly fascinating to each new generation seeking to identify the forces that shaped their world.

Seven Hundred Years of Change

The time that historians call the Middle Ages, beginning in A.D. 771, when Charlemagne was crowned king of the Franks, running to 1461, when Charles VII of France died, was a time in which kings held on to their power by force of arms. A king's ability to hold or expand his territory depended on how many men would pledge their loyalty to him personally. Historians refer to authority of this sort as suzerainty. With bravery and strength of character, the ruler, or suzerain, led his fighters into battle, enlarging and keeping his kingdom together through invasions, raids, and self-defense.

Personal attributes like strength of character were crucial in the suzerain's ability to command the loyalty—and arms—of his subjects. In later times a ruler might appeal to a sense of national identity among his subjects; the king of France, for example, might reasonably expect his subjects to fight on behalf of France. A suzerain of the Middle Ages, by contrast, usually ruled a patchwork of lands separated by territory belonging to another suzerain or by a large body of water—such as the English Channel. The suzerain's subjects might speak any of a half dozen mutually unintelligible languages or dialects, but when he asked them to, they would fight on his behalf—and if they refused, he would very soon cease to rule.

To the victorious suzerain went not just the spoils—that is, the lands and wealth of whomever he defeated. The victor could also demand, and fully expect to receive, the loyalty and service of the loser's fighting men. So it was that a ruler of the Middle Ages could generally count on conquered territory staying that way—unless a rival suzerain invaded and was victorious.

And invade they did. During the Middle Ages, rulers generally considered battling neighboring suzerains to be one of their main jobs. The harsh winter climate in Europe generally made the movement of armies impossible, so the summers were the season

The Middle Ages

The great rulers and major events of this era

Charles VII
(1403–1461)

Charles VII created a strong central government in France.

Edward III
(1312–1377)

Edward III united and ruled England for fifty years.

King Louis IX of France ruled with compassion for the poor and loyalty to the Christian church.

Louis IX
(1214–1270)

Genghis Khan and his Mongol warriors created the world's largest empire.

Genghis Khan
(1167–1227)

As emperor, Frederick I frequently battled against disloyal areas of the Holy Roman Empire.

Frederick I
(1122–1190)

William the Conqueror won the Battle of Hastings to become king of England.

William the Conqueror
(1028–1087)

Charlemagne was the first to unite the Holy Roman Empire.

Charlemagne
(742–814)

Hundred Years' War 1337–1453

1500
1492 Columbus lands in America.

1461 Charles VII dies.

1431 Joan of Arc murdered.
1400

1360 Treaty of Brétigny
1347 Bubonic Plague

1300

1273 Hapsburg Dynasty established.

1232 China uses gunpowder in battle.
1200

1176 Frederick I defeated in northern Italy.

1147 Second Crusade

1100
1096 First Crusade

1066 Battle of Hastings

1000 Vikings land in America.

800

771 Charlemagne crowned king.

700

Middle Ages

A medieval suzerain leads his knights into battle to defend his territory from an invading army.

for fighting. For months at a time, a ruler such as Charlemagne would be on the borders of his realm, either trying to expand his territory or defending it from others. So it was that men like Charlemagne, William the Conqueror, Frederick Barbarossa, Genghis Khan, Louis IX, Edward III, and Charles VII spent substantial portions of their lives in battle. In fact, given the possibility that a ruler would be killed in battle or receive an injury that would eventually cause his death, these seven rulers are unique in the extraordinarily long and productive reigns they enjoyed. They generally ascended to their respective thrones as teenagers and lived, on average, to the age of sixty-two. Such an age was considered remarkable, far longer than the average peasant could expect to live. These were, indeed, remarkable men whose actions changed the face of a continent and in ways large and small continue to matter more than five hundred years after the end of the era known as the Middle Ages.

CHAPTER 1

Charlemagne: Making Empire Holy

From his youth, Charles (or Charlemagne, as he was later known), the long-lived king of the Franks and ruler of the Holy Roman Empire, saw power as belonging to the strong in battle. That power, Charles believed, existed for a purpose: to uphold his faith. In the process, Charles deeply influenced the course of history, making possible what people today know as European civilization.

A Frankish Christian

Charles was born in 742, in that part of the old Roman Empire known as Christian Gaul (or Frankland). Charles's mother was known only as Bertha. His father, Pépin the Short, was mayor of the palace of King Childeric III. For all practical purposes, Pépin was in charge of Childeric's kingdom because he also was in charge of the king's military.

Although his father ran the Frankish kingdom, Charles had little prospect of inheriting great power. That changed, however, when Pépin took the throne for himself, forcing the king to enter a monastery. A fierce defender of Christianity, Pépin vanquished so many pagan feudal lords that in 751 the pope legitimized his usurpation and had him crowned by a papal envoy. Charles's prospects were improved still more by his betrothal to Himultrud, the daughter of Desiderius, king of Lombardy, which lay on the other side of the Alps.

Upon Pépin's death in 768, Charles and his younger brother, Carloman, each inherited half of the Frankish kingdom. Carloman died three years later, leaving Charles, at age twenty-nine, the responsibility for ruling the whole kingdom. Even in faraway England historians noted Charles's ascent, recording in *The Anglo-Saxon Chronicle* that 771 was "the beginning of the rule of King Charles."[1]

Family Life

At the beginning of his reign, Charles married Himultrud, forming an alliance between the Franks and the Lombards. But Charles

soon showed that he did not take the alliance as seriously as he did his need for a healthy heir. When Himultrud bore a severely deformed son, Charles asked the pope to annul the marriage. The pope went along, leaving him free to marry someone else, even though it ended the alliance with Lombardy.

Charles's desire for a healthy heir was fulfilled. His second wife, Hildegarde, bore him nine children, including three sons, before she died in 783 at the age of twenty-five. His third wife, Lady Fastrada of Franconia, raised Hildegarde's children along with the three daughters she bore. After her death in 794, Liutgard became Charles's fourth wife.

Charlemagne became ruler of the Frankish kingdom in 771 after the death of his father and brother.

Summers in Frankland

King Charles lived the life of a Frankish warlord. Just as his father Pépin had done, the king spent his summers warring against neighboring feudal lords. As he annexed the lands of these vanquished lords, he gained the authority to call their men to military service. This was common feudal practice, and as cultural historian François Louis Ganscholf explains: "All the subjects of the king, even peoples recently subjugated . . . owed him military service."[2]

Since many of these vanquished rivals were pagans, Charles soon became known to the Christian Franks, and to the pope, as their protector. Historian Maurice Keen writes, "Later epic was not wrong essentially, in portraying him leading the forces of Christendom against heathen enemies."[3]

Winters Among the Franks

If Charles's summers were spent in military campaigning, his winters were spent hunting and traveling from one feudal court to another. This was a way for Charles to collect what was owed him by his vassals. Keen explains this practice: "Given the expense and difficulties of transport, it was often easier for the lord to come to the estate and reside there for a time with his followers, to consume his plenty on the spot rather than have it sent him."[4]

This seasonal traveling suited Charles. The winters gave him the chance to get better acquainted with his vassals. He also loved hunting and bringing home game to feed his growing family and enjoyed the company of other fighting men.

In 781 Charles added the fostering of learning to his winter activities. He built a palace school for his children and a beautiful church, called Aix-la-Chapelle, at his residence at Aachen in northeastern Frankland. He brought great scholars to his school. One of them, named Alcuin, got Charles interested in studying Latin. Although Charles himself never really mastered the books,

Charlemagne visits with students in his palace school. The school attracted the brightest scholars from all over Europe.

he liked to have others read to him and discuss with him Roman writers such as Virgil. Over the years Charles's school trained scholars who fanned out across the European continent, in effect introducing literate people to ancient literature and paving the way for what later became known as European civilization.

The Conquest of the Lombards

Charles remained a warrior, however, and in the early 770s found himself having to defend his earlier decision to break his alliance with Lombardy. The Lombard king, Desiderius, invaded Rome. The pope called on Charles, as defender of Christianity, to come to his rescue. Charles, accordingly, fought his way through Lombardy, deposed Desiderius, and took the Lombard throne himself. That winter he brought Queen Hildegarde and her six living children with him across the Alps to spend Christmas in the Lombard capital, Pavia.

Charles's takeover of Lombardy benefited him in two ways. It enlarged the lands from which he could collect his feudal dues. More importantly, from Charles's point of view, the conquest gained him new titles, and with them political power. After June 6, 774, writes Ganscholf, "His title was 'Charles, by the grace of God, king of the Franks and the Lombards, as well as a patrician of the Romans.'"[5]

Pope Adrian I asks Charlemagne to protect Rome from the invading Lombards. Charlemagne defeated Desiderius, king of Lombardy, and took control of his kingdom.

The Campaign in Spain

Charles now moved to expand his defense of Christian Frankland. He marched into battle against the Muslims who had for decades occupied the Spanish kingdom of Cordova. *The Anglo-Saxon Chronicle* recorded his successes in battle: "Charles entered Spain. . . . Charles destroyed the cities of Pamplona and Saragossa, joined his army, and having received hostages and subjected the Saracens [Muslims], returned to the Franks through Narbonne."[6]

Charles's campaign in Spain ultimately failed, however. He conquered only the most mountainous northern region, called Gascony. Then, on the march home through the mountain chain known as the Pyrenees, following their limited victory, Charles and his army were attacked. The unsuspecting Franks suffered a humiliating ambush in a narrow pass controlled by the natives of the region, known as Gascons. Biographer Allen Cabaniss recounts the attack:

> At a signal [the Gascons] attacked the train [military caravan] without warning. The rugged terrain, the heaviness of the Frankish armor, and the lightning speed of the Gascon assault rendered the rear guard helpless with no opportunity to make a stand. In short order the Gascons had hurled them from the precipice into a deep gorge. In the failing twilight the Gascons plundered the richly laden train and scurried away into the night. Charles discovered in dismay and too late that he could not avenge this insult and defeat.[7]

The Annexation of Saxon Territory

Following this defeat, for all practical purposes Charles gave up the idea of taking territory south of the Pyrenees. Instead, he devoted his summers to campaigns in the roadless wilderness to the east of Frankland. In the summers of 775, 776, and 777, he led the Franks in successful defenses of Frankish vassals against cross-border raids by the non-Christian Saxons.

Each time he defeated the Saxons, Charles attempted to make peace by Christianizing them in mass baptisms. But the Saxons broke the treaties they made under these circumstances. Biographer Robert Folz writes that Charles realized his periodic efforts would not solve the problem of the Saxons' raids:

> As an independent country, Saxony was too great a danger to the Frankish state, and from now onwards a policy

Charlemagne leads his troops into battle against Muslims occupying the Spanish kingdom of Cordova. Charlemagne's foray into Muslim Spain proved disastrous.

of conquest seemed imperative, all the more so as it appeared the only way of assuring the triumph of Christianity in northern Germania. At this point there began a series of cruel, relentless annual expeditions. . . . In 785 [the Saxon leader] Widukind finally surrendered.[8]

Following Widukind's surrender, Charles deported many of the vanquished Saxons to the unpopulated parts of other subject kingdoms, such as Franconia and Alemania. He also continued to expand his influence by pushing farther and farther east, establishing overlords loyal to himself throughout the area. All in all, Charles spent nearly thirty-two years annexing country north to the Baltic Sea, south to the Adriatic Sea, and east nearly to the Black Sea.

Church and State

During this time a change took place in the way Charles ruled. His previous style had consisted of allowing local lords to rule their lands as they wished; now his style slowly began to mirror that of the popes, who, in Roman fashion, stressed greater direction from the top. To make certain that administrators, both the civil magistrates and the bishops who oversaw religious matters, carried out their duties in a standardized way, Charlemagne visited them personally, punishing neglect and misbehavior. As early as 774, the pope, Adrian I, gave Charles a collected volume of church laws; Charles, Folz writes, drew "largely upon it for his own legislation; thus indirectly was the Roman order established in the Frankish kingdom."[9]

Charles's personal presence, then, affected all his vassals, and his abilities were soon extolled by all who knew him. One avid admirer in particular wrote frequently in praise of his accomplishments.

Masons cut stone for a church under Charlemagne's watchful eye. Charlemagne took a personal interest in the affairs of his kingdom, and he often met with administrators in person.

This was Alcuin, head of the school at Aachen, who wrote of him in flowery terms as "[a suzerain] whose right hand wields the sword of triumph, and whose mouth trumpets forth the sounds of Catholic piety."[10]

As a Christian ruler, Charles emulated the Christian virtue of caring for the poor. His biographer, Einhard, who knew him personally, writes, "Wherever he heard of Christians living in poverty, he would send them money out of compassion for their wretched lot, even overseas, to Syria and Egypt, as well as to Africa, Jerusalem, Alexandria, and Carthage. This was also the chief reason why he cultivated friendships with kings across the seas."[11]

Such friendships expanded both Charles's influence and his personal wealth. For example, Harun, king of Persia, allowed Charles to send offerings to the Christian shrines of Jerusalem and then sent back Persian treasures. Einhard reports:

> [Harun] the king not only permitted [Charles's representatives] to carry out their mission but also gave Charles the jurisdiction over [the supposed site of Jesus's burial, known as the Holy Sepulcher]. On their return Harun sent along his own messengers with precious gifts, garments, spices, and the riches of the Orient. A few years earlier Charles had asked him for an elephant and Harun had sent him the only one he owned.[12]

Meeting the Pope

Charles's continuing policy of helping the pope now took on greater significance. In April 799 some of Pope Leo III's Roman subjects rebelled, and the pope himself was taken prisoner. Escaping, however, as the result of what he claimed was a miracle, the pope traveled to Saxony, where he met with Charles and asked for protection.

Charles decided to open an enquiry into the attack and examine the case in person. The next year he made a trip to Rome to carry out his mission as well as to make a pilgrimage to his favorite church, St. Peter's Basilica. This visit, in 800, was his fourth trip to the center of Christianity, for, says Einhard, "of all the sacred and holy places, he loved the Cathedral of the Holy Apostle Peter . . . most of all."[13]

The pope, meanwhile, sought to associate himself with Charles's power by arranging an added ceremony for Charles that traditionally would only have been accorded an emperor. Folz describes the scene of his arrival:

Pictured is St. Peter's Basilica in Rome, built in the 1500s on the site where Pope Leo III crowned Charlemagne Holy Roman Emperor on December 25, 800.

> [Riding] horseback, in the midst of a distinguished procession, [Charles was met] with waving banners and accompanied by the acclamations of the crowd lining his route, . . . all the way . . . to the square in front of St. Peter's. Leo III . . . was waiting for him at the top of the steps and led him into the basilica to the accompaniment of psalms.[14]

Charles then held a weeklong enquiry into the rebellion of 799. At the end of his investigation Charles declared that those who had attacked the pope were guilty of rebellion, but that they should be pardoned. On December 23, 800, in return for having been restored to the papal throne, Pope Leo III followed up on his elaborate welcome and addressed a gathering of church officials. He proposed that Roman influence and prestige be restored by naming Charles Holy Roman Emperor. The whole assembly agreed, says Folz, and proclaimed that "[He] was marked out by God to be chosen by the bishops and the Christian community [who] deemed it fit and proper that the imperial title should be conferred upon Charlemagne."[15]

Christian Emperor

Charles, or Charlemagne, as he was thereafter known, was crowned emperor in Rome on December 25, 800, by Pope Leo III. Donald A. Bullough describes the event:

> The king was kneeling in prayer before the tomb of [Saint Peter, having] taken off the crown he wore on special occasions, together with his weapons and other insignia. As he rose the Pope placed the crown upon his head and an obviously well-rehearsed section of the congregation chanted three times. . . . "To Charles, the most pious Augustus, crowned by God, the great and peace-giving Emperor, life and victory."[16]

Now Charles carried even greater moral authority. Imperial acts after 800 included written regulations naming obedience to

Emperor Charlemagne addresses a group of nobles in this illustration. Charlemagne relied on his prestige as emperor to command the respect of his vassals in his far-flung kingdom.

the emperor a Christian duty. This applied to both lay persons and clergy. He even instituted an oath of fidelity for his knights, which made it a mortal sin to switch sides in a conflict.

Power in the Empire

Being declared emperor meant that Charlemagne no longer needed to go out on summer campaigns. The lands that today comprise France, Germany, and the northern half of Italy, along with the lands north of the Adriatic Sea, paid him tribute. To unify and administer this enormous empire, Charlemagne could now rely on his own prestige to assure that his personal emissaries would be received and the instructions they carried would be heeded.

In any situation that required his presence, Charlemagne made the most of his personal bearing. His contemporary, the biographer Einhard, describes the emperor in his mature years:

> Charles had a big and powerful body and was tall but well-proportioned. That his height was seven times the length of his own feet is well known. He had a round head, his eyes were unusually large and lively, his nose a little longer than average, his gray hair attractive, and his face cheerful and friendly. Whether he was standing or sitting his appearance was always impressive and dignified. His neck was somewhat short and thick and his stomach protruded a little, but this was rendered inconspicuous by the good proportions of the rest of his body. He walked firmly and his carriage was manly, yet his voice, though clear, was not as strong as one might have expected from someone his size. His health was always excellent, except during the last four years of his life, when he frequently suffered from attacks of fever. And at the end he limped with one foot.[17]

Charlemagne's authority remained undiminished even as he weakened physically. He had no opposition, therefore, when he made known the way he planned to divide the empire among his three sons, Louis, Pépin, and Charles.

Last Years

Though the emperor rarely traveled in his last years, there continued to be other travelers who spread the word of his greatness. These were the court entertainers, called troubadours, whom he often brought in to entertain at court events. Essentially serving as historians, the troubadours went from court to court recounting

Charlemagne's exploits in chansons de geste ("songs of valor"). One favorite chanson de geste, *The Song of Roland*, told of the bravery of one of Charlemagne's favorite warriors, who was killed during the ambush of the army in the Pyrenees.

Charlemagne's plans for dividing his kingdom were undercut as he outlived his sons Pépin and Charles. As his own death approached, the emperor made final arrangements for his successor. In 810 his grandson Bernard, age fifteen, was declared ruler of Lombardy, Corsica, Sardinia, and Bavaria. In 813 Charles's one surviving son, Louis, was crowned Holy Roman Emperor. Another grandson, Charles II, became king of the Franks.

Charlemagne died on January 28, 814, brought down by complications of pleurisy, a painful inflammation of the chest. "His body," writes Einhard, "was washed and prepared for burial in the custom-

Charlemagne ruled for nearly fifty years, and some historians credit his rule as the start of modern European civilization.

ary way, then brought to the basilica and buried amid the great lamentations of the entire population."[18] At Aix-la-Chapelle, his favorite place, his epitaph read, "Beneath this tomb lies the body of Charles, the great and orthodox Emperor, who nobly increased the kingdom of the Franks and reigned prosperously for forty-seven years."[19]

Legacy

In a relatively short time, Charlemagne's division of territory among his heirs hardened into regional boundaries that would define power struggles in Europe for hundreds of years to come. Yet despite these divisions there lingered among the people a tendency to identify with the shared values Charlemagne had promoted. Thus, "in some sense," as Allen Cabaniss writes, "European civilization was launched by Charlemagne."[20]

CHAPTER 2

William the Conqueror: Holding on to Power

William I of England was a man driven to seek power. From the time he became Duke of Normandy at age eight, he rarely hesitated to use force, whether it was to settle a quarrel between competing vassals or to collect the taxes owed to him. When, at age thirty-eight, he won the English throne, there was little doubt that William deserved the title "the Conqueror." Proud and bold, he imposed Norman rule on England, in the process unifying the people and creating in them a common identity as Englishmen.

Unhindered by Illegitimate Birth

The child who would grow up to conquer England was born in humble circumstances in 1028. His mother, Arletta, was a village leather worker's daughter. His father, however, was Robert I, Duke of Normandy, a cousin to kings and queens as well as other contenders for the thrones of England, Scotland, and Denmark.

In Normandy's class-conscious society, the humble standing of William's mother meant that she would never be accepted as duchess. Accordingly, Robert arranged her marriage to a wealthy friend of his, who raised William along with his own two sons, Odo and Robert of Mortain. Despite his son's illegitimate birth, the duke was able to persuade his peers to accept William as his heir to the dukedom. With his successor chosen, Robert I departed, joining in a crusade to free Jerusalem from occupation by Muslims. Robert died in 1034, not ever having returned home, and William became Duke of Normandy. The boy was just eight years old, and there were plenty of would-be rulers who would stop at nothing to eliminate the young duke. Historian David Armine Howarth writes, "The guardians Robert had appointed for his son were poisoned or stabbed by one faction or another or thrown into dungeons, and for years, to save his own life, he was hidden and moved from place to place by his mother's family."[21]

As William matured, he came to believe that he was not only destined to rule Normandy but also much, much more. William's

William became duke of Normandy after his father's death in 1034. The life of the young duke was constantly threatened by conspiracies hatched by would-be rulers.

cousin was King Edward of England. In 1041 William paid his royal cousin a visit, in the role of vassal to his more powerful relative. No record exists of what the two discussed, but afterward William said that Edward promised him the crown of England. When William was knighted in 1042, and frequently afterward, he made a point of mentioning his future glory.

For the time being, however, William had his hands full, for the situation in Normandy continued to be chaotic. As he dealt with continual small-scale rebellions on the one hand and attempted to expand his own power on the other, William was mentored by his overlord, King Henry I of France and by Baldwin, Count of Flanders. Fighting side by side with them in one major revolution in 1047, William decisively overcame powerful foes such as Philip of Anjou, Guy of Britanny, and the Count of Maine. With the support of his mentors, then, William emerged as Normandy's most powerful warrior.

William found support of a different sort when, in 1051, he married Count Baldwin's daughter Matilda, whom he had courted for seven years. Beyond proving a loyal wife and mother, Matilda also showed that she was capable of wielding power on William's behalf during his frequent campaigns to defend or expand his domain.

William, shown in this illustration as his army lands on the English coast, built a reputation as a very brave and powerful warrior long before he invaded England.

Through his exploits, William's reputation for bravery and zeal in battle grew. His manner and appearance added to his success. Historian Kenneth M. Setton gives his characterization of the tall, well-built William: "[He was] resolute and resourceful, avaricious, rarely humorous, always unsentimental, [and] found life a serious business. He expressed practical ideas in a grinding tone of voice."[22]

The Loyalty of the Norman Knights

William's battles also added to his military forces. This was because each time he overcame a foe, the defeated feudal lord had to accept William's right to call up men for future service. When he was still in his twenties William had eight hundred knights pledge to fight for him when called upon to do so.

The loyalty of William's knights depended, however, on his standing with the church. Although knights took an oath to be faithful to their feudal lord, that oath also committed them to serve God and protect Christendom. A feudal lord who failed to stay in the church's favor did so at great risk of losing his grip on power. Howarth notes how the duke went about winning and holding that favor:

> William himself could not rule without the support of the church; so he defended it strongly and earned its blessing. He presided at its synods, approved or disapproved its laws and appointed its bishop . . . some [of them] members of his family who would do as they were told—most notable among them his half-brother Odo, who was as warlike as any Norman.[23]

In addition, William showed himself faithful by building churches, endowing abbeys, and ingratiating himself with individual clergymen. In particular, he gained the ear of a certain intelligent and eloquent Norman abbot, a friend of the pope named Lanfranc.

William's Prospects in England

Meanwhile, William clung to his expectation of one day ruling England. That prospect was strengthened in 1064, when King Edward's brother-in-law Harold arrived in Normandy. Historians disagree on whether this visit was purely accidental—the result of Harold's being shipwrecked—or if Harold had been sent by King Edward on a diplomatic mission. In any case, William and Harold struck up a friendship, and at some point Harold pledged loyalty to William, an indication, says Howarth, that "William was making the best of a chance that put Harold in his power."[24]

A scene from the Bayeux Tapestry depicts Harold, the son of the King of England, swearing an oath of allegiance to William.

Harold's pledge to William, however, proved meaningless. Two years later, on January 5, 1066, King Edward died. The next day, the king's council, called the witenagemot, offered Harold the throne, saying this had been Edward's wish. Harold accepted and was crowned.

Taking Up the Challenge

William was determined to fight for what he believed was owed him. Yet for him to raise an army to win the English throne, says Howarth, "[he] needed very wide support, in Normandy and outside it; and as soon as he made up his mind what to do he had to invent other motives, or allow them to be invented for him."[25] William, in other words, needed to sell his plan to potential supporters. Even though his knights were pledged to follow him, William knew they had to be convinced the effort was worthwhile. To them, William made the invasion of England sound like a road to riches.

William also needed the church's blessing, and so he tried to make the invasion seem like a moral undertaking, a just punishment for Harold having broken his pledge of loyalty. William even sent his longtime friend and adviser Lanfranc, recently risen to new prominence in the church hierarchy, to present his case to the pope. In her article "The Norman Conquest Through European Eyes," Elisabeth van Houts writes, "Abbot Lanfranc had drawn up the Norman case, of which the main argument was that Harold had committed perjury and that therefore the duke was justified in using violence against him. The Pope, a friend of Lanfranc . . . happily gave his blessing to William's enterprise and . . . sent him a papal banner as a sign of his approval."[26]

North of the English Channel

Other support was soon forthcoming. Setton writes, "The great feudal lords of Normandy soon pledged their support for an invasion of England to help their duke secure the throne. He lost no time in preparing for the tasks ahead."[27]

Throughout the spring months, both William and Harold gathered forces and supplies on their respective sides of the English Channel. Over the summer they kept watch, William for a favorable wind to take his ships to England, and Harold for sight of a hostile fleet. But, unknown to either one, a third party was about to enter the fray. This was Harold's brother Tostig. Also determined to claim the English throne, Tostig had convinced the king of Norway to invade northern England in support of Tostig's claim. Immediately responding to this threat, Harold marched north, and on September 25, 1066, his forces defeated those of the Norwegian king.

The Battle of Hastings

As luck would have it, just three days later the winds William's sailors had been awaiting began to blow. On September 28 William's fleet sailed across the English Channel, landing near the town of Pevensy. After a day of foraging, William's forces moved east to Hastings, where his men set up camp.

Harold soon heard of William's invasion, but he was powerless to prevent the Norman forces from gaining a foothold. After a three-day forced march back to London to gather replacements, Harold resumed the march sixty-five miles farther to the south to confront his foe.

Drawn up outside of Hastings on October 14, 1066, the opposing armies were approximately the same size, with seven thousand troops each. However, William could clearly see that Harold was better situated since his forces were on a hill. William overcame this disadvantage by directing his bowmen to aim high so that their arrows would fall on the heads of the English troops. What came to be known as the Battle of Hastings was short but bloody. It ended when Harold died, his eye pierced by an arrow.

The news of Harold's death and the Norman victory traveled rapidly to London, and the Londoners sent a delegation of diplomats to meet William and negotiate terms of surrender. *The Anglo-Saxon Chronicle* reports, "[William] promised to be a gracious lord to them."[28] He was crowned William I of England on December 25, 1066, in Westminster Abbey.

In France, William's half brother, Bishop Odo, commissioned skilled needleworkers to commemorate William's victory in em-

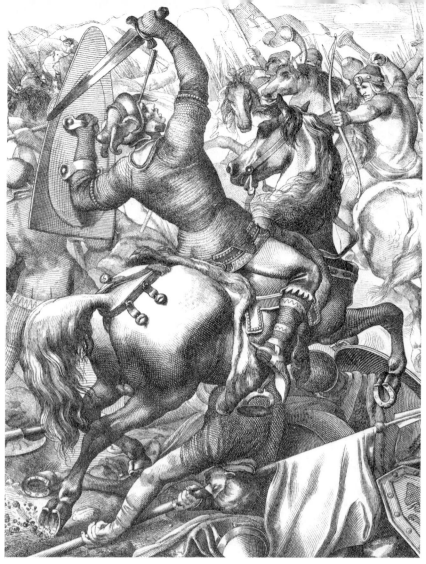

William and his troops defeat Harold on October 14, 1066, during the Battle of Hastings. After his victory, William assumed the throne and took control of Anglo-Saxon England.

broidery on seventy-seven yards of linen, which came to be known as the Bayeux Tapestry. Among the tapestry's images of knights dressed in helmets and chain mail is an image of the proud William, his head thrown back, exclaiming, "Look at me well! I am still alive and by the grace of God I shall yet prove victor."[29]

After the Conquest

William moved quickly and with a strong hand to impose Norman rule over England and its Anglo-Saxon majority. The contemporary writer Odericus Vitalis describes the new ruler's actions: "The native inhabitants were crushed, imprisoned, disinherited, banished and scattered beyond the limits of their own country; while [William's] own vassals and adherents were exalted to wealth and honors and raised to all offices of state."[30]

Three years after the Battle of Hastings, no one disputed his rule. As biographer Maurice Ashley notes, "William was an extremely experienced ruler, administrator, and commander, having been for over twenty years in full charge of his duchy."[31]

William's triumphs went beyond England's borders. Over the next five years he led expeditions into the north and south of England and in 1069 through 1070 even into Wales. He returned to Normandy and turned back a renewed challenge by Philip of Anjou, who was now king of France. William also resisted invasions by the Danes and defeated the Scots in 1072, signing a treaty with their king, Malcolm III. Clearly, as historian Setton writes, "he lived his greatest—and his worst—moments on the battlefield."[32]

William continued to work to earn approval from the church. In England, as he had done in Normandy, he built churches, abbeys, and schools. Lanfranc, now head of the English church as the archbishop of Canterbury, along with other scholars, taught philosophy, theology, and Christian dogma. Over time, William's support for learning drew large numbers of scholars to England.

The Salisbury Oath and the Domesday Book

William's hold on England was firm, but he sought to assure that his heirs would one day enjoy similarly unquestioned authority. In 1082 he set out to accomplish this by requiring all important landholders to take a loyalty oath. To make it clear that loyalty would also be owed to his son Henry, Duke of Salisbury, the oath was administered in Salisbury, thus becoming known as the Salisbury oath. The oath also included a promise that the barons would pay their feudal taxes on their property.

To assure that all those owing taxes would indeed pay what was due, William decided that he needed a complete record of his English lands. Thomas B. Costain, in *The Conquerors*, narrates William's proposal of this comprehensive survey of England:

> At a midwinter assembly . . . the king made a long speech. He was concerned, he said, about the condition of the country, the confusion brought about by so many wars, the lack of knowledge which existed of population and wealth. "By the splendor of God!" exclaimed William at

the conclusion of his address . . . , "We must know all about this land and what it contains. Today we know nothing."[33]

William's general survey of England and its landownership was accomplished with great speed and accuracy. This record, known as the Domesday Book, ensured complete and thorough collection of taxes. Costain tells how the information was gathered and why it is deemed to be so important:

The nation was divided into nine districts, and a special commission was appointed for each. . . . The commission

William accepts the crown in front of London's Westminster Abbey, where he was crowned King William I of England on December 25, 1066.

Pictured is a page from the Domesday Book, a comprehensive survey of England and its landownership commissioned by King William.

moved about the territory assigned to it and all landowners and tenants were summoned to attend their meeting. Every man was questioned minutely, and the information he gave was later checked to insure honesty and accuracy. How much land did he hold? Who held it before he became the owner? How many people resided on it, and what was their condition? How many horses did he have, how many cows, sheep, goats? . . . The result was the Domesday Book, the document from which more than from any chronicle or history the truth about England at the start of Norman rule has been gleaned.[34]

Last Days

Meanwhile, the situation in Normandy was deteriorating. In 1083 William's wife Matilda died, and their oldest son Robert announced that the title Duke of Normandy belonged to him, even though his father was still alive. Robert went so far as to make an alliance with Philip of Anjou, king of France and longtime foe of William. To defend his right to rule Normandy, William fought his son, repeatedly defeating his forces and even making inroads into lands belonging to the French king himself.

One challenge William had to deal with was the loss of Mantes, a town on the River Seine. In 1087 William laid siege to Mantes, defeating those who were holding it. The battle for Mantes was William's last. He had burned the town and was riding through the ruins when his horse stepped on a smoldering plank and threw him off. In great pain, he was taken to a nearby monastery, where he lay dying for over a month.

In those last weeks, looking back over his life as a soldier and a ruler, William came to repent what he now saw as his sins and failings in his reign in England. He prayed for forgiveness for his harshness, saying, "I persecuted the native inhabitants of England beyond all reason. Whether nobles or commons [common people], I cruelly oppressed them; many I unjustly disinherited, innumerable multitudes, especially in the county of York, perished through me by famine and sword. . . . I am stained with the rivers of blood that I have shed."[35]

As William lay dying, he also made known his wishes regarding his lands and crown. He bequeathed Normandy and Maine to his eldest son, Robert, and England to his younger son William Rufus. He provided Henry with treasure with which to purchase his own sovereign territory.

William died on September 9, 1087, at the priory of Saint Gervais. He was buried at Caen in St. Stephen's Church, which he had built.

William's Legacy

Historians generally agree that William's conquest of England brought about considerable fusing of Norman and Anglo-Saxon

This engraving inaccurately depicts William dying shortly after being thrown from his horse. In truth, William languished for more than a month before dying on September 9, 1087.

culture and language. In addition, because of Norman rule, English and continental politics became evermore intertwined. Wars on the continent became increasingly important for England, particularly when France was involved. Perhaps of greatest significance was the unity of purpose the Norman Conquest and rule brought to the English people. Costain writes, "With the coming of foreign kings, and their stern conceptions of law enforcement, the country drew together. . . . A boon the Normans brought."[36]

CHAPTER 3

Frederick Barbarossa: Imperial Justice

Frederick I, known as Barbarossa, looked and acted his part as a Christian military hero. Ambitious, even to the point of cruelty when defending the Holy Roman Empire, Frederick was, nevertheless, concerned with maintaining peace among his feudal lords. Committed to asserting his authority, he alternately led crusaders to the Holy Land and supported a rebel faction of the church.

A Steady Rise to Power

Frederick I, born in 1122, was descended from two powerful feuding families of the Holy Roman Empire, which at that time stretched from northern Germany to central Italy. His father was Duke of Swabia and part of the Hohenstaufen dynasty, which had its center of power in Germany. His mother, Judith, was of the Welf dynasty, which was centered in Italy.

Broad-shouldered and muscular in build even as a youngster, Frederick was educated in the arts of politics and war. The boy was, however, less interested in theory found in books than in learning the physical skills a leader needed, such as horsemanship. Frederick's uncle, Conrad III, became Holy Roman Emperor when Frederick was sixteen years old. Conrad hoped that his young nephew would one day succeed him; since the boy represented the uniting of the two dynasties, Conrad believed that in his young heir would end the destructive feud.

Besides being Holy Roman Emperor, Conrad III was also king of Germany. This was a difficult role since, far from being a distinct nation, Germany was really just a patchwork of duchies whose feudal lords constantly battled one another. Young Frederick soon found himself involved in these disputes when his father retired to a monastery, leaving the young man essentially in charge. Frederick joined his uncle in trying to quell these disturbances. Biographer Marcel Pacaut says, "Fighting by his uncle's side . . . Barbarossa was able to see at close quarters how these petty rivalries undermined the authority of the crown, and prevented the king from governing the country. It was a lesson he never forgot."[37]

Frederick's appreciation of a ruler's need to exert authority developed further when he accompanied his uncle in an attempt to wrest control of the Holy Land from Muslims, known as the Second Crusade. The Crusade was a failure, serving as a lesson in how bad management leads to defeat. Conrad's troops were undisciplined, and after several shattering losses, the crusaders returned home in discouragement. The Crusade, says Pacaut, "gave [Frederick] further proof, if such was still needed, that only a king with great personal authority could hope to enforce discipline."[38]

King of Germany

Five years later, as it became clear that Conrad III was nearing the end of his life, the German princes gathered for the election of the next king of Germany, who would also be in line to become Holy Roman Emperor. Conrad forcefully denounced the ongoing family feuding and called attention to Frederick's extraordinary abilities. Frederick's biographer-uncle, Otto of Freising, explains:

> The princes, therefore, considering not merely the achievements and the valor of the youth [Frederick], . . . but also this fact, that being a member of both [the Hohenstaufen and Welf] families, he might—like a cornerstone—link these two separate walls, decided to select him as head of the realm. They foresaw that it would greatly benefit the state if so grave and so long-continued a rivalry between the greatest men of the empire for their own private advantage might by this opportunity and with God's help be finally lulled to rest.[39]

Conrad III died on February 15, 1152. Less than three weeks later, on March 4, 1152, Frederick was crowned king of Germany. He was thirty years old and a committed Christian who held as his ideal the maintenance of peace in his homeland. Frederick's biographer Otto of Freising, describes the new king:

> Now divine, august Frederick is . . . shorter than very tall men, but taller and more noble than men of medium height. His hair is golden, curling a little above his forehead. His ears are scarcely covered by the hair above them, a barber (out of respect for the empire) keeps the hair on his head and cheeks short by constantly cutting it. His eyes

Frederick was crowned king of Germany in 1152. He immediately set out to suppress conflicts between feuding nobles in his domain.

are sharp and piercing, his nose well formed, his beard reddish, his lips delicate and not distended by too long a mouth. His whole face is bright and cheerful. His teeth are even and snow white in color. The skin of his throat and neck . . . is milk-white and often suffused with the ruddy glow of youth; modesty rather than anger causes him to blush frequently. His shoulders are rather broad, and he is strongly built. . . . His gait is firm and steady, his voice clear, and his entire bearing manly.[40]

In this eighteenth-century painting, Holy Roman Emperor Frederick is wed to sixteen-year-old Beatrix of Burgundy.

Frederick set out to restore unity among the princes of Germany. Starting with the western duchies, he led battles against and made concessions to Hohenstaufen nobles. Then he proceeded to put down the feuding Welf nobles who were ravaging the country. He overwhelmed his Welf cousin Henry the Lion and in general worked to end the private wars between feudal lords that were plaguing Germany. The new king quickly entered a swirl of political intrigue between the pope, the Byzantine emperor, and various European monarchs. Combining political savvy with military might, Frederick marched through northern Italy and on June 18, 1155, was crowned Holy Roman Emperor by Pope Adrian IV.

Frederick's own political skills were supplemented the next year, when he married sixteen-year-old Beatrix, daughter of Count

Rainild of Burgundy. As queen and later as empress, she proved to be an amazing woman, one who accompanied him on his campaigns and negotiated many favorable alliances. Beatrix also bore Frederick eight sons and three daughters.

Designs of Power in Unity

A diligent administrator, Frederick traveled constantly to see that the nobles honored his commands. Hoping to establish allies on Germany's borders, Frederick installed a new leader loyal to himself in Poland in 1157 and invaded Bohemia in 1158. His contemporary biographer Rahewin, who continued the work of Otto of Freising, observes, "Frederick . . . let no days pass in idleness, thinking those lost on which he had not made some enactment . . . for the preservation of law and justice among all peoples."[41]

Practical Problems

Frederick was now emperor, but his crowning produced two practical problems he had not foreseen. First, by allowing the pope to physically place the crown on his head, Frederick had acknowledged that the pope's authority was greater than his own. Second, during his march to Rome, Frederick had weakened the defenses of numerous cities, leaving them vulnerable to invasion.

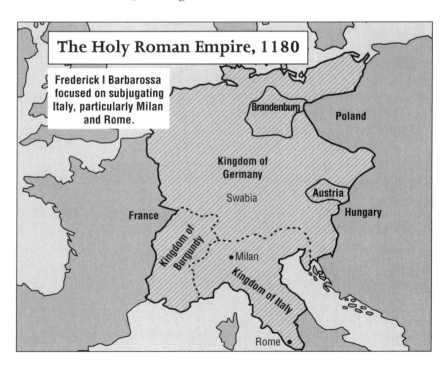

The Holy Roman Empire, 1180

Frederick I Barbarossa focused on subjugating Italy, particularly Milan and Rome.

Brandenburg

Poland

Kingdom of Germany

Swabia

Austria

France

Hungary

Kingdom of Burgundy

• Milan

Kingdom of Italy

Rome •

He took different approaches to these two problems. He ignored the cities' vulnerability, but he actively denied the pope's supremacy, going so far as to appoint a number of bishops—a right the pope claimed for himself alone.

Taking Sides

The pope reprimanded Frederick, and in response, Frederick led an armed force directly to Rome.

During the conflict the pope died, and a period of instability followed as various papal candidates jockeyed for position. At various times two different men claimed to be the rightful leader of the church. The search for a new pope also reignited the old rivalry between the Hohenstaufens and the Welfs. Despite his long-standing determination to end the feud, Frederick was drawn into it as he supported a Hohenstaufen over a Welf candidate. Frederick was again forced to take sides in the feud as he tried to establish imperial control over northern Italy, where various cities sided either with the Hohenstaufens or the Welfs. So it was that when an envoy from the Hohenstaufen-controlled city of Cremona came to him pleading for help in repelling an attack from Welf-allied Milan, Frederick agreed to defend Cremona. An anonymous poet describes the righteous stance Frederick took:

> [The envoy's] speech caused tears to flow down
>   Frederick's cheek.
> He gave his handsome head a shake and spoke:
> "I see Milan must be restrained by force
> To keep the peace and to preserve our laws,
> Which often love of power made her spurn.
> It hurts me to have heard all those complaints
> And yet not give to poor men some relief.
> Unless they give up war and show contrition,
> We'll make those evil people pay their debt.
> They'll learn too late the power of the king."[42]

The Destruction of Milan

The emperor made his intentions of attacking Milan clear, in keeping with the rules of war that were widely observed at the time. Those rules also obligated Milan's leaders to provide a guide who was supposed to show Frederick a place where his army could camp and prepare for battle. Milan's leaders, however, ordered the guide to lead Frederick's army to a wasteland where there was no food for his men or forage for the horses. The emperor was infuriated. Otto of Freising writes, "He was moved to anger and turned his arms against the people of Milan, saying, 'Do I not sit on my throne, renowned and attended by a great force of valiant soldiers? Shall a Roman emperor be forced against his will to be anyone's purveyor and not his benefactor?'"[43]

In response to this treachery, Frederick burned Milan. The ruined city was barred from coining money, had to pay heavy fines, and was forced to give up three hundred hostages to assure continued compliance with Frederick's commands. Milan had to permit the emperor to build an imperial castle in the center of town.

Confident of his control over Milan, Frederick sent most of his army home. But his cruel attack and harsh occupation had aroused great hostility, to the point where rebels attempted to assassinate him. The emperor barely escaped to Germany.

The End of Imperial Power in Italy

Despite the assassination attempt, Frederick remained determined to impose his imperial will on the Italian cities and to force the pope to recognize his supremacy. To accomplish these goals he once again invaded Italy, capturing Rome in 1167. Frederick's victory did not accomplish his objectives, however. A combination of local resistance to his authority and an outbreak of plague forced the emperor to retreat. Frederick made two more attempts to bring Italy

Christian soldiers march into battle during the Crusades. Emperor Frederick led an army across Turkey to fight in the Third Crusade, but he died along the way.

under his control and to force the pope to acknowledge his supremacy, but these invasions were also unsuccessful. In the end, an alliance of northern Italian cities, known as the Lombard League, defeated Frederick's forces at the Battle of Legnano in 1176.

Thereafter, Frederick ended his campaigns in the north of Italy and made peace with the Lombard League. Scholars say, however, that the emperor was inclined to give up his quest for supremacy even before this turn of events. Peter Munz writes, "The [peace] treaty was not the result of a military defeat. It was the result of Frederick's determination to change his whole policy and to end the years of indecision."[44]

Reconciliation with the Church

Emperor Frederick I returned to Italy yet again, but this time he did so with the goal of reconciling with the church. In Venice on July 24, 1177, Frederick prostrated himself before the pope and publicly acknowledged his fault: "Let it be known to the entire world that although we are clothed in the dignity and glory of the Roman Empire, this dignity does not keep us from human error; imperial majesty does not preserve us from ignorance."[45]

As part of this reconciliation, the pope lifted the excommunication that he had imposed on Frederick years earlier when the emperor had recognized Victor IV rather than Alexander III as pope. His regaining of the pope's favor strengthened Frederick, enabling him to make peace with the Lombard League on favorable terms. Marcel Pacaut writes, "[Frederick] eliminated his rival[s] in strict accordance with feudal law and with the full approval of his princes."[46]

In May 1184 Frederick's hopes of asserting imperial authority, even in church matters, came to fruition. The pope accepted his invitation to hold a meeting of the universal church in the autonomous city of Mainz on the Rhine River. Pacaut writes, "He presided over the Diet [international assembly of bishops] of Mainz, the most triumphant and splendid of his entire career. Here a multitude of princes and foreign envoys witnessed the knighting of his two elder sons, Frederick and Henry."[47]

The Third Crusade

Frederick was now moving into old age. His reign of thirty-eight years had witnessed his participation in countless military battles and five major campaigns across the Alps on horseback. Scholars regard the emperor's accomplishments as remarkable. At the very least, writes Munz, "given the primitive technology of the period,

Throughout his life, Frederick I was committed to defending the Holy Roman Empire. The empire itself survived until the nineteenth century.

41

the poor horses and the bad roads and the very imperfect conditions for resting on the way, Frederick performed during these thirty-eight years a tremendous physical feat."[48]

One last, tremendous effort was to be Frederick's. In early December 1187 the emperor listened to his bishop's impassioned plea to recapture Jerusalem from the Muslims who were in control of the city and its holy sites. He made preparations for what would be his last military venture by leaving the empire in the hands of his capable son, Henry VI.

Frederick never reached the Holy Land. Eager to get started, he set out on an overland route through what today is Turkey rather than wait for the ships belonging to his French and English fellow crusaders. On a hot day in September 1190, with the city of Seleucia in sight, he went ahead of his army to refresh himself by the River Saleph. Munz writes, "Whether it was the sudden shock of the cold water or the strong current which was too much for Frederick's strength, he drowned. His men tried to reach him, but when they dragged him to the bank, Frederick was dead."[49]

Emperor Frederick's sudden death dispirited his army. Deprived of his leadership, the crusaders, now led by the English king, were able only to negotiate a three-year truce that guaranteed pilgrims safe travel to visit the holy sites and gave a portion of the Palestinian coast to the Christian invaders.

Legacy

The Holy Roman Empire that Frederick idealized survived until the 1800s, though with little practical impact. In Italy, the northern cities' support of each other against Frederick's attacks proved the forerunner of national unity. In Germany, however, Frederick's imposition of peaceful settlements among feuding families, combined with strong princes and an ever-deepening sense of local loyalty, fragmented the kingdom into smaller and smaller duchies. Not until the late nineteenth century would the dreams of the man who for thirty-eight years firmly and unflinchingly promoted German unity be realized. Legends of Frederick Barbarossa abounded, however. One legend says, "He is not dead, but, seated between six knights at a table of stone, he sleeps in the Thuringian mountains."[50]

CHAPTER 4

Genghis Khan: Inflexible Conquest

Mongol general Genghis Khan, says Willard Price in *National Geographic* magazine, was "the greatest troublemaker of ancient Asia."[51] This ambitious member of a nomad tribe was far more than that, however. Genghis Khan used his extraordinary organizational powers and military genius to rise from obscurity and raise an army that maintained a strong presence all across Asia and eastern Europe. At the head of this army, he amassed and administered an empire greater in area than any other the world has known.

The Son of a Mongol Chief

The boy who would become the emperor Genghis Khan was born sometime between the years 1162 and 1167, about eight hundred miles northeast of Beijing, China. His father was Yesügei, a Mongol chief of the nomadic Borjigin tribe. His mother, Höelun, had been abducted from a hostile Merkit tribe, called the Unggirats. Named Temüjin ("Iron-smith") by his parents, he was the eldest of their five children.

Temüjin spent his first eight or nine years on the sparse grazing land of the Onon River headwaters region. The boy grew up in traditional fashion, riding herd on the livestock of his family and learning the legends and customs of the Borjigin. As was customary among Mongol tribes, he was taken at about age eight to the Unggirat tribe of his mother to be betrothed. His bride-to-be, born of a prominent family, was Borte ("Gray Eyes"). After the betrothal, his father departed, leaving Temüjin with the Unggirats to learn their customs.

Temüjin's time with the Unggirat tribe was short, however, because his father went home through the lands of his enemies the Tatars. Somewhere along the way, he was poisoned and quickly died. Yesügei's death left his wife Höelun and his children destitute. Temüjin was brought back to help them. There was little Temüjin could do, however. Biographer Leo de Hartog describes

Genghis Khan was a fierce warrior who carved out and administered the largest empire in world history.

their difficult situation: "There followed a hard time for the bereaved family. It was understandable that the Borjigins found Temüjin too young to accept him as the head of the clan. The circumstances in which the Mongols lived were too rigorous for a boy to be able to lead them."[52] De Hartog goes on to note that Höelun and her children were subjected to unusual hardship: "It is not clear [however] why the Borjigin clansmen deprived Höelun's

family of a large part of their possessions and then left them behind when the clan moved elsewhere. Yesügei's abandoned family
had to try to survive in the country around the source of the Onon
[River] by hunting and fishing."[53]

Temüjin led his younger siblings and their mother as they faced
constant danger, insisting that they must stay together. When the
Merkits stole the family's few horses, they survived in the barren
Onon River canyons only by their ingenuity and toughness.

Temüjin and Jamuqa

Sometime during these years of constant movement, Temüjin met
another young nomad, Jamuqa of the Jaijirat tribe. So close did
Temüjin and Jamuqa become, writes biographer de Hartog, that
"the two became brothers bound by oath (anda-brothers, or blood
brothers)."[54]

The Secret History of the Mongols provides the words the two
young men exchanged in the sworn oath of brotherhood:

> I [shall be] a faithful companion,
> reminding him of things that he has forgotten
> and waking him [when] he has slept.
> I shall become the whip of his chestnut horse,
> and never fail to answer to our summons.
> I shall not break rank.
> I shall campaign for him in distant places
> and fight for him close by.[55]

*Men travel on horseback across a desolate snowy plain in Mongolia.
Genghis Khan helped his nomadic family eke out a spare existence in the
harsh Mongolian landscape.*

Tribal Conflicts

Over the next few years, Temüjin began to feel he could exert the authority he was rightfully entitled to as the son of a warrior chieftain. He was considered old enough to marry, so one of the first steps he took in claiming what was due him was to return to the Unggirats to claim Börte.

The trip did not go as planned. On the way home, while Temüjin was hunting, Börte and her servant woman were spotted by some Merkits. They rode off with the women, saying, "To avenge the abduction of Höelun, we will carry off their women. We have taken our revenge." [56]

The young Genghis hides as guards search for him during an abortive attempt to rescue the captive Börte from members of the Merkit tribe.

Temüjin was captured while trying to rescue Borte. He escaped and evaded recapture and sure death by lying submerged in a cold stream. All of his pursuers but one, a young man named Jelme, missed his hiding place. Admiring Temüjin's endurance, Jelme kept his secret and Temüjin retained his freedom.

Within a few months, and with Jamuqa's help, Temüjin boldly returned, entered the Merkit camp, and rescued Borte, who by now was pregnant. When she bore a son, Temüjin accepted the boy as his and named him Jochi ("Guest"). The author of the article "The Canonization of Genghis," writes, "Temüjin was a thoughtful husband and a good father. He was married at 15, and though his was an arranged union . . . he seems to have grown fond of his bride."[57] Temüjin and Borte had three sons of their own, Ogödei, Chagatai, and Tolui, who would one day become great generals and warriors in their own right.

The Mongol Tribes Are United

The young Mongol now began in earnest to assert the warrior authority he had inherited from his father, Yesügei. In charge of thirteen thousand men by Jochi's second birthday, he instilled loyalty among his followers by rewarding those who did his bidding with more authority. Another successful practice in Temüjin's rise to power was to unite several tribes in a common effort. Of like mind in the forming of alliances was his blood brother, Jamuqa, who was also rising in status among the Jaijirat. By joining in battle, their two tribes together defeated the Merkits.

From this experience, Temüjin and Jamuqa grew to believe that all the Mongol tribes should be united. By forming such a union the Mongols would be better able to defend themselves and eventually would be able to control the network of trade routes between China and Europe that historians call the Silk Road.

Temüjin and Jamuqa's first approach to the Keraits, the tribe that controlled the trade route, was successful. Once the Keraits, who were converts to Christianity, were persuaded that Temüjin respected other religions and would not persecute the Christians, they became Temüjin's allies.

Grand Khan of the Mongols

Between 1204 and 1206, Temüjin and Jamuqa united all the Mongol tribes in the region of the Onon River. In 1206 they all gathered in a great assembly and proclaimed Temüjin to be Genghis Khan ("Great Warrior"). The anonymous *Secret History of the Mongols* recounts the tribes' ritual of subjecting themselves to another's rule. Their oath was something like the oath of blood brothers:

> We will hunt the wily beasts
> and round them up for you.
> We will squeeze together the animals of the steppe for you
> until their bellies touch.
> We will squeeze together the animals of the cliff for you
> until their thighs touch.
> On days of battle,
> should we disobey,
> then separate us
> from our precious family and our property,
> from our qatuns and wives,
> casting our black heads
> onto the ground.
> In days of peace,
> should we ignore your counsel,
> then exile us
> from our men and servants,
> from our wives and children,
> and cast us out into the wilderness.[58]

This binding oath allowed Genghis Khan to assemble an army so fierce in battle that other tribes would voluntarily surrender, since the alternative was extermination.

The Parting of Genghis and Jamuqa

One person in the Mongol army began to be envious of Genghis's success. This was Jamuqa, who began to assert that the Jaijirats—and he as their chieftain—ought to have control of all the Mongols.

In his introduction to *The Vinland Map and the Tartar Relation*, Alexander O. Victor summarizes the blood brothers' conflict by quoting a Mongol proverb: "There are a sun and a moon in the sky, but there cannot be two kings on earth."[59]

Jamuqa persisted in his effort to gain power, although he knew Genghis too well to think there could be compromise. *The Secret History of the Mongols* records that during one of their encounters, Genghis realized, "If I now say 'Let us be companions,' you will reject my offer. If I try to spare your life, you will not wish [me to do so]." Genghis Khan went on to vow that he would kill his rival without shedding his blood, decreeing "that his bones should not be abandoned in the open but buried decently."[60] Genghis Khan kept his word, had Jamuqa smothered, and then buried him.

The Program Expands to the South

As the new khan's ambition grew, mastering northern Mongolia became but a first step to conquering all of the Gobi Desert lands to his south, east, and west. With only one objective in view, he forced tribe after tribe to pay him homage. This was a strategic effort, as Adam T. Kessler writes: "He was not an impulsive conqueror, but, rather, a cunning and highly organized master of his domain."[61]

The Mongol leader was ready by 1211 to invade northern China. Less than two years later, Genghis Khan and his army breached the massive wall that had been built to protect the Chinese Empire against earlier Mongol attacks.

Despite his coming as a conqueror, Genghis Khan found easy acceptance among the Chinese. The invaders soon harnessed the resentment ordinary Chinese felt when they contrasted their own poverty against the wealth and luxury in which their emperor lived—luxury supported by oppressive taxes. The emperor went into permanent exile, and the khan's extended occupation lasted until 1234.

A Truly Formidable Army

The army with which Genghis Khan took over China was a military machine of unsurpassed quality. Exacting strict obedience from his generals, the khan now began to train larger and crueler forces for further conquest. Even hunting parties became opportunities to practice for swift raids and lightning retreats.

Genghis Khan leads a large force of heavily armed soldiers into China. His army was one of the most fearsome military units in history.

The army's gear gave them great mobility and potency. Military analyst J.H. Liddell Hart gives some details of how the khan equipped his seemingly invincible army: "They had three quivers, each with a different caliber of arrows for the various ranges. One class could penetrate armor, and the other was suitable against unprotected troops. In addition, their light artillery consisted of various missile-throwing machines, mangonels, and catapults."[62]

Kessler describes what was expected of the fighters:

> The Mongol warrior was robust, capable of riding days on end and nourishing himself without cooked food. He consumed dried milk curd, millet meal, and meat that he cured by placing it under his saddle and drank blood from an incision cut into the neck of his horse. When the army paused to hunt, the men would eat dogs, wolves, foxes, horses, rats, mice, lice, and even the afterbirth of their mares.[63]

Not only did the khan have a well-disciplined and well-equipped military, but he chose his generals wisely. He trained them in following orders to the exclusion of personal benefit. And he continued his system of granting to the best of them ever greater authority. In his book *Great Captains Unveiled*, Hart writes, "Merit and not seniority was the key to advancement."[64]

Forging Farther West

Having subdued northern China, Genghis Khan began the plundering of cities along the trade routes between Asia and Europe. As he progressed farther and farther west, he established a network of way stations where horses could be fed or fresh horses obtained.

In 1219, just five years after the Chinese emperor had fled his capital, Genghis Khan began a three-year conquest into western Asia by leading his first great excursion into Khorasmia, northeast of the Caucasus mountain range. From 1220 until 1222, his fighters, who valued only what they could carry off, pillaged the Crimean ports on the Caspian sea and raided communities in what today is eastern Poland and northern Hungary. Only when the northwestward-moving army reached the Volga, north of Moscow, was it turned back by fighters who had survived earlier Mongol raids and who practiced many of the same tactics the khan used.

Drawn by the prospect of even more treasure, the army forged farther and farther west. Aided by accurate intelligence and close relationships with old allies along the Silk Road, the Keraits,

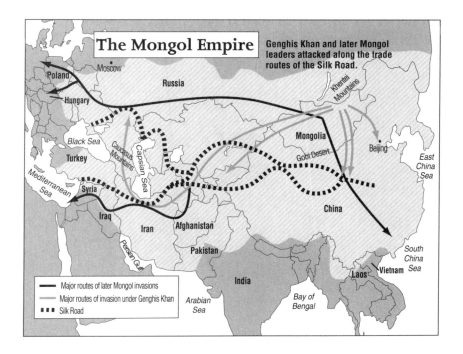

The Mongol Empire

Genghis Khan and later Mongol leaders attacked along the trade routes of the Silk Road.

— Major routes of later Mongol invasions
— Major routes of invasion under Genghis Khan
••• Silk Road

Genghis Khan's trusted general Subatai reached the Dnieper River and its mouth on the Black Sea, thus commanding a trade route leading to the Baltic Sea. By controlling this route, the Mongols had the opportunity to capture loads of furs, ivory, fish, ropes, iron, antlers, and timber. Thus, they completed their virtual control over northern access to both the Black Sea and the Caspian Sea and uncontested plundering of the Silk Road, with its constant traffic in silk, spices, brocade, and jewelry.

Invasion of the Middle East

Genghis Khan's last conquest was also his boldest. In 1222 he set his sights on Nashapur and Samarkand, between the Hindu Kush in Afghanistan and what today is Iraq.

The khan set up an important camp at Lake Balkash and prepared to cross the Caucasus Mountains (between the Black Sea and the Caspian Sea). In the three separate attacks he organized, he used false retreats so successfully that the shah was totally unprepared for the Mongols' final attack in fall 1222 on the capital, Samarkand. Hart writes:

> Rarely, or ever, in the history of war has the principle of surprise been so dramatically or completely fulfilled. . . . Every move [was] made in calculated and orderly sequence to-

This illustration pictures Genghis Khan in sumptuous dress. The Mongols grew incredibly rich through regular plundering of trade routes such as the Silk Road.

wards the gaining of the ultimate objective, those purposeful moves being finally crowned by the tremendous surprise appearance from the Kixyl-kum Desert in the Shah's rear.[65]

Learning to Settle Down

In the winter of 1222–1223, Genghis Khan remained in his newly conquered territory south of the Caucasus. There, he learned about living in a less severe climate and in more civilized surroundings, where farmers could grow fruits and grains and people did not constantly have to move their flocks to find pastures.

Genghis Khan's experience of Persian civilization rendered him ready to listen to those councillors who suggested effective ways of actually ruling the vast territory he had invaded, raided, terrorized, and plundered. That summer, upon his return to Mongolia, he instituted schools in the capital, Karakorum, and promoted the education of his people. He instituted an eastern and a western chancellery where men loyal to him ruled in his name. His decrees were spread by word of mouth and in the form of written documents. These decrees were given the force of law by the possibility of swiftly organized military occupation and the systematic slaughter of all military-age males or even of entire villages.

Looking to the Future

In the over twenty years of Genghis Khan's rule, his sphere of influence spread from Beijing in China's north and Shantung on the Yellow Sea to the Volga and the territory southwest of the Black Sea and north of the Mediterranean. After his return from his conquests, he lived in relative quiet for a few years, enjoying the spoils of war, although he himself did not adopt the lavish lifestyle he had observed among Persian rulers. Thinking of the future of his empire, he strove to ready his sons to carry on his great work. In doing this he relied on displays of anger and the invoking of tradition to shame them into complete subjection to authority, even in seemingly insignificant matters. *The Secret History of the Mongols* records how he responded in the manner of a traditional Mongolian patriarch when his sons came to him with a request:

> After hearing their petition, [Genghis Khan] calmed down and granted [his] three sons Jochi, [Chagatai], and [Ogödei] an audience. He reprimanded them, citing old men ['s] words, quoting ancient words, until they almost sank into the ground on which they stood and were unable to wipe the sweat from their brow. He shouted [at them] in admonition.[66]

By ruling through his sons and generals and maintaining a network consisting of mounted couriers, Genghis Khan kept track of everything that went on in his empire. Inflexibly dispensing punishment to anyone displaying disloyalty or cowardice, he held undisputed sway over the greatest empire in history.

The Khan's Final Years

One of Genghis Khan's greatest worries was that his empire would fall prey to squabbling between his sons. He was particularly worried that Jochi, because of his uncertain parentage, would be attacked by his half brothers. As it happened, Jochi, who was not healthy, died in February 1226. The khan then made it clear how responsibility for ruling the empire would be divided. Chagatai

An engraving shows Genghis Khan on his deathbed attended by a servant (left) as he divides the territories of his empire among his three sons. The khan's sons expanded his empire even farther into Europe and the Middle East.

would defend the southern kingdom south of the Himalayas; Tolui, the central plains; and Ogödei, the eastern provinces.

In the end, what for a young man would have been a relatively minor accident proved to be the khan's undoing. Aged sixty, he led a successful campaign against rebels in the far east on the north end of the Yellow Sea. "During a battle," writes de Hartog, "Genghis Khan's horse was startled and reared unexpectedly, the old world conqueror fell and was injured. His condition worsened so much during the night that [his sons and generals were called and told] that he had a heavy fever."[67] Genghis Khan died on August 18, 1227, surrounded by his family.

The news of Genghis Khan's death was kept a secret. Nobody, moreover, was to know where the great khan's final resting place was. According to Kessler, "Mongol legend recounts that all creatures, human and animal, all that encountered the funerary procession on its journey quickly were executed to ensure that his tomb would not be discovered and looted."[68]

The Legacy of Genghis Khan

During the twenty years of his conquests, Genghis Khan amassed an empire greater than that of any other conqueror the world has known. His military and organizational genius, acknowledged by historians as superior to that of such revered strategists as Napoléon, was not only proven but was carried on by his successors. Although the khan's sons held the huge portion of Asia he had taken over and, aided by his generals, expanded even farther into Christian Europe and the Middle East, it was Genghis Khan's genius that made all that possible. Biographer de Hartog writes, "It is no exaggeration to claim that his genius lay primarily in his talent as a general, his knowledge of men and his ability in organization. These three qualities were to make him one of the greatest leaders in the history of the world."[69]

CHAPTER 5

Louis IX: The Idealistic Monarch

From early in his life, the ideal of the boy who became King Louis IX of France was to seek what was right and just. Brought up by his mother, Blanche of Castile, to fear God, Louis remained a religious man throughout his long reign. As a king, he was devoted to justice for all his subjects, but especially for the poor. He displayed bravery in taking on the defense of Christians when they were under attack in the Holy Land, embarking on two Crusades to do so. To his contemporaries, as well as to many modern-day historians, Louis IX was and is the epitome of morality and rectitude.

Heir to the Throne

Louis IX was born in 1214 in Poissy, France, to Prince Louis VIII and Princess Blanche of Castile. His family lived a quiet life of privilege, knowing that Louis VIII would one day be king and that his son would one day succeed him.

France's crown came to young Louis sooner than expected, for Louis VIII died after just three years on the throne. When he was crowned in Rheims in 1226, Louis was tall and mature for an eleven-year-old. Yet though her son already looked the part of a king, Blanche worried that his feudal lords would try to win easy favors from the young king. She therefore saw to it that self-serving lords were not allowed to jockey for Louis's favor. Biographer Marion A. Habig writes, "Blanche administered . . . with such impartial justice and great wisdom that the envious were silenced."[70]

Louis slowly took over the government for himself. His marriage to Margaret of Provence, on May 29, 1234, marked his coming of age and the time when he really began to rule in his own right.

A Pious Knight

In carrying out his royal responsibilities, Louis modeled his behavior on that of a knight. He rode tirelessly to battle against rebels, such as those who besieged Poiteau in 1241. In 1242 he led his knights against King Henry III of England, who was invading Normandy. These campaigns show, says a study by historians Daniel Borzeix, René Pautal, and Jacques Servat, that "Louis IX was . . . a man of war who . . . on this occasion completely dispossessed the king of England."[71]

King Louis IX of France gives thanks to God after taking the city of Damietta from the Saracens. Throughout his life, Louis modeled his behavior on the ideal of the devout knight.

Louis also set an example of knightly values. He gave money to the building of churches and established Toulouse University to teach church doctrine. He collected sacred manuscripts and multiplied the holdings of abbey libraries. He supported the abbeys where artists copied and illuminated bibles and prayer books. He prayed and went to mass often. In order to intensify his devotion, he collected items directly connected to Jesus and the saints. One of these treasured relics was a sliver of wood that had supposedly come from Jesus' cross.

Called to the Seventh Crusade

Given such a devout attitude, it is perhaps not surprising that Louis paid close attention to sermons in which priests spoke of the difficulties Christians were experiencing in the Holy Land, where Muslim warriors had attacked Jerusalem. By 1246 Louis felt inspired to help defend the holy places of Christendom, where the pope called for crusaders to turn back the attackers and restore peace.

Louis's mother and his advisers all tried to dissuade him. According to Régine Pernoud, they said that "the King should place the duties of state before his personal feelings."[72] Even the bishops questioned his decision. According to biographer Winifred F. Knox, they asked, "To whose care can you commit your weak and desolate subjects?"[73] His answer was to put his kingdom in the charge of his mother, Blanche, who, even at sixty years of age, remained able to command the respect and obedience of her son's subjects.

Over the next two years Louis spent vast sums equipping one hundred ships and gathering thirty-five thousand men. On August 25, 1248, Louis, Queen Margaret, and their children, along with the crusaders, departed from southern France. Their destination was Damietta, located in the Nile delta in northern Egypt. From this staging area, Louis hoped to launch an attack from the sea, hitting the Muslims holding Jerusalem from behind.

A Religious Journey

Because the Crusade was undertaken in the service of God, Louis insisted on good behavior aboard ship. Says his contemporary biographer, Jean de Joinville, "Louis never tolerated cursing or sinful conversation either among the servants or among the courtiers."[74]

The conviction that his mission was serving God gave Louis courage. At one stage of the voyage his ship suffered the loss of twenty feet of its keel, torn off on a sandbar. The king was advised to leave the ship and its passengers and let the sailors row

During the Seventh Crusade, Louis IX leaps from a ship onto the Egyptian shore. After taking Damietta, Louis prepared to make an assault on Muslim-controlled Jerusalem.

him ashore. He refused to leave, telling the five hundred people on board to pray. He said, "I would rather place myself, my wife, and my children in God's hands."[75]

When the ship and people were saved, Louis told one of his retainers:

> You know, seneschal [steward], God has manifested His great power quite plainly to us, in that one of His little winds—not any of the four major ones—has come near to drowning the king of France, his wife and children, and all his company. We are therefore bound to show our gratitude and give him thanks for delivering us from such peril.[76]

Taking Damietta

The perils, however, were only beginning. Louis's plan was to winter on the island of Cyprus, to wait for the arrival of crusaders from other lands, and then attack Damietta. After a delay caused by the late arrival of the additional men, Louis and his crusaders sailed on to Egypt. In spite of the fact that it was oppressively hot there, they overcame a small force of defenders and captured Damietta on June 4, 1249. The crusaders then established a camp where they could prepare for the assault on Jerusalem.

The king chose February 1250, hot weather and high water time on the Nile, to begin the advance toward Jerusalem. Leaving a contingent to guard Damietta, Louis's ships set sail, wending their way through the waterways of the Nile delta, their destination the coast of Palestine.

Louis's decision proved to be a bad one. The crusaders' ships were soon separated from each other among the twisting channels of the delta. By this time, a Muslim army had gathered along the shore, close enough that their arrows could reach the ships. The crusaders were overwhelmed. Those who survived, including Louis, were taken prisoner.

Louis's massive army comes ashore in Egypt, and prepares to march on Damietta.

At the same time another Muslim force attacked Damietta. The guard panicked, but Queen Margaret, who was soon to give birth, rallied the men to order. The Muslims, moved to mercy by her personal pleas, ceased the attack. They also set the terms of Louis's release. The Muslims demanded that Louis either pay a ransom or renounce his faith. Biographer Habig tells of the king's response to the proposed agreement:

> The king replied: "Such blasphemous words shall never cross my lips." They threatened him with death. "Very well," said he, "you may kill my body, but you will never kill my soul." Filled with admiration at his steadfast courage, they finally released him without the objectionable condition.[77]

Negotiator in Palestine

Given his freedom, however, Louis did not go home. His military venture was at an end, so he tried to accomplish his objective by means of personal diplomacy. He went from city to city trying to persuade various Muslim leaders to leave Jerusalem in peace. Over the next six years he traveled around Palestine, negotiating truces, strengthening fortifications, establishing barricades, and trying to salvage some advantage for the Christians.

Louis's efforts largely failed, and he was forced to abandon his project entirely when word reached him that his mother, Queen Blanche, had died. But he never gave up his ideals. Throughout the six years he spent in Palestine, says biographer Margaret Wade Labarge, "even in dealing with the Saracens, the king would not countenance any dishonesty."[78]

Historians note that although the Seventh Crusade failed in its main objective of freeing Jerusalem from Muslim occupation, it benefited Louis in other ways. His high morals, along with his valor, earned him respect among the knights and nobles of France. Knox says, "The Crusade was a sound policy for the King. . . . Louis only went out to battle as the servant of the Cross, but he came back, more certainly than ever before, the king of France."[79]

A Repentant Man

In 1254 he marked his return by moving the center of his government to more sumptuous quarters in Paris. He should have been comfortable and happy. Still, the failure to free Jerusalem from Muslim domination gnawed at him. Simon Lloyd writes, "Louis returned home a changed, even haunted man. He was convinced that

Louis IX is held hostage in Palestine after being captured by Saracens. Impressed with his steadfast character, Louis's captors released him unharmed.

it was his sins that had led to disaster, interpreting his captivity and humiliation as just, divine punishment. . . . His new outlook was reflected in changes to the outward trappings of his lifestyle."[80]

At first, Louis's preoccupation with what he considered to be his personal moral failings led him to consider doing penance as a monk. Queen Margaret, however, convinced him not to follow this impulse. Eyewitness Joinville provides some details on the compromise Louis arrived at:

> He never wore ermine or squirrel fur, nor scarlet cloth, nor were his stirrup or his spurs gilded. His clothes were made of camlet or grey woolen cloth; the fur on these or on the coverings of his bed was either deerskin, hare-skin,

or lambskin. He had such sober taste in food that he never ordered any special dish for himself, but took what his cook prepared, and ate whatever was put before him. He had water mixed with his wine and drank it from a glass goblet, with more or less water according to the strength of the wine. . . . He always took care to see that his poor were fed and, after they had eaten sent money to be distributed among them.[81]

A Kind and Fair Judge

Louis upheld the right of his poorest subject not to be mistreated by landlords. He set up court in the city of Vincennes and in other centers, and, as king, he heard complaints. Even serfs could appeal to him personally to examine what they felt to be unjust decisions of local judges.

In the end, Louis's reforms actually benefited the landlords. His insistence that peasants not be abused gave farmworkers hope of —if not actual prosperity—at least making a living. As a result, the productivity of France's peasants and the lands they farmed improved. Biographer Albert Guérard takes the position that this is what made Louis a great ruler: "France remembers him under the oak at Vincennes dispensing justice to the humblest, a wise and fearless ruler. Not to magnify his office but because he desired justice, he interceded directly throughout the kingdom."[82]

Relatives in Spain and England

Even as King Louis strengthened his position at home, he worked to extend France's power by settling long-running international disputes. With Spain, for example, Louis negotiated the Treaty of Corbeil in May 1258. Under the terms of this agreement, Louis gave up Barcelona and Urgel south of the Pyrenees. In return, Toulouse and a number of other cities on the northern slopes of the Pyrenees came under Louis's rule.

Of greater significance was Louis's settlement of old disputes with England. Since the time of William the Conqueror, the English kings had exercised feudal rights over territories in France. It followed that, particularly along boundaries between French and English possessions, there was constant friction. These squabbles were made even more painful to Louis by the fact that Queen Margaret's sister Beatrice was the wife of Charles of Anjou and her sister Eleanor was Henry II's queen in England. With his in-laws at odds, as Knox writes, "Louis' orderly mind had always wished for a definite legal settlement between the two countries."[83]

By May 28, 1259, Louis had worked out a trade with Henry II. In the Treaty of Paris, Louis obtained suzerainty over Normandy, Anjou, Touraine, Maine, and Poitou. In return, he gave up suzerainty over Gascony with its fertile vineyards. When he was criticized for the Treaty of Paris, Louis answered, "It seems to me that I get a good exchange for that which I gave to the King of England. For he was not my man before, and now he becomes one of my vassals."[84]

Louis's Religious Zeal

The sense of justice and fairness that so advantaged much of France did not, however, extend to those who held religious views at odds with church doctrine. Under King Louis, church officials, known as inquisitors, freely prosecuted heretics. Writes Labarge, "An ordinance, made in the name of Louis . . . laid down the provisions for the search and punishment of heretics. The civic penalties were extreme: no heretic could make a will or inherit, and all his goods were to be confiscated with no possible reversion to his heirs."[85] Large number of heretics, who were considered dangerous, were burned at the stake.

Jews also suffered under Louis's decrees. Historians Borzeix, Pautal, and Servat write, "The ordinance of 1269 prescribed that the Jews distinguish themselves from the Christians by a yellow scarf or by fastening a four-inch [piece of] felt on their clothes. [And] Louis IX ordered that their books be burned."[86]

Emissary to the Mongols

The zeal that led to such persecution remained undimmed in the king, and Louis never forgot that the Holy Land remained in the hands of Muslims. Therefore, when he heard that Muslims had dealt yet another defeat to Christians of the Byzantine Empire (successor to the eastern half of the Roman Empire), he returned again to the thought of evicting the Muslims from the Holy Land. This time he had reason to hope that he had a potent new ally. The Mongol ruler Kublai Khan had begun to attack Muslim interests east of the Jordan River, and it seemed to Louis that the khan might help free Jerusalem from its Muslim occupiers.

Louis dispatched an emissary to the Mongol chief, proposing such an alliance. Kublai Khan's reply, however, was not only discouraging but openly threatening: "We advise you to send us a sufficient sum of money in yearly contributions for us to remain your friends. Otherwise we will destroy you, as we have destroyed other kings."[87]

King Louis serves a meal to the poor in this illustration. Louis exhibited tremendous compassion for his poorest subjects.

The Last Crusader King

The refusal of Kublai Khan to join forces against the Muslims only temporarily dampened Louis's crusader spirit. Louis determined to make one last attempt to free Jerusalem. He gave over control of his kingdom to his oldest surviving son, Philip, and, accompanied by three other sons and two of his brothers, Louis set off on another crusade.

But Louis's final effort to regain the Holy Land for the Christians was doomed from the start. Some of the knights accompanying Louis were interested mostly in what they could gain in material wealth. Rather than work together to achieve religious goals, each pursued his own interests. Typifying this attitude was the king's own brother-in-law, Charles of Anjou, king of Sicily, who considered their ally Byzantium a threat to his own power. Historian Maurice Keen writes, "The fatal inconsistency which ruined the expedition was clear from the first. Louis was fired by missionary zeal, his army by desire of conquest."[88]

Throughout the ordeal the king had to deal with the knights' hopes for self-aggrandizement and with the typical discomforts and illness. Winifred F. Knox writes, "Food began to run short. . . . Fever and enteric [intestinal disease], those inveterate enemies of the European in such a climate, attacked the army."[89] Louis remained a model crusader and military leader. He put his own needs last and the needs of his soldiers first.

Following the death of many of his knights and soldiers, one of his own brothers, and one of his sons, John Tristan, Louis himself came down with chills, fever, diarrhea, and vomiting. On August 25, 1270, Louis IX died in Tunis, in northern Africa, far from the Holy Land he had so long hoped to regain for Christianity.

King Louis's bones were returned to Paris and were buried at the Abbey of Saint Denis. His epitaph reads, "To whom will the poor now carry their plea, since the good king is dead, who loved them so much."[90]

Louis's Legacy

Louis's death in Tunis ended crusading fervor in France. Lloyd writes, "His death in some sense marks the end of an era in the history of the crusading movement, for Louis' expedition to Tunis proved to be the last of the great international crusades . . . [for] the recovery of the Holy Land."[91]

Louis IX's main legacy was a period of peace and prosperity for France. Continuing gains in agricultural productivity resulted in plenty of food, and as peasants felt more secure, their overlords prospered as well. Louis's son Philip III respected the words his father had written on his deathbed:

> You must give your attention to ensuring that your subjects live peaceably and uprightly under your rule. Above all maintain the good cities and communes of your realm in the same condition and with the same privileges as they

A nineteenth-century painting depicts the death of Louis IX in Tunisia. The king was canonized in 1297 and he is known to posterity as Saint Louis.

enjoyed under your predecessors. If there is anything in them that needs reform, do what is necessary to set it right and keep them ever in your favor and your love.[92]

Louis's personal attention to any and every citizen set a precedent that would not always serve the people's interests. In the hands of a less benign monarch, highly centralized power could easily turn to despotism. Yet for centuries to follow, monarchs were judged by the example of kindness and fairness that Louis IX set.

CHAPTER 6

Edward III: Princely and Popular

King Edward III's skill in leadership allowed him to rule England for fifty years. A tireless fighter and organizer, brave on the battlefield, and politically deft, Edward mobilized his people behind his military efforts. Despite the vast expenditures required by the war he started with France, one of the longest and most destructive Europe had known, Edward died a popular king of a united England.

King Edward III, renowned for his military courage and political strategy, ruled England for fifty years.

Parents in Conflict

The offspring of rulers of the two most powerful kingdoms of Europe, Edward III was born on November 13, 1312, to King Edward II of England and Queen Isabella of France, whose marriage had been intended to unite their countries. But the boy who would one day inherit England's throne had in Edward II a poor role model since the king showed only indecisiveness and spent much of his reign warring with his own nobles.

Edward learned from his mother, Queen Isabella, how to act decisively. When young Edward was eleven, she took him to France, raised an army there, and, on September 27, 1326, invaded England and forced her husband into exile. By October 26, 1326, King Edward II was apprehended and imprisoned, and Parliament gave his son Edward III the honorary title guardian of the kingdom.

Prince Edward, meanwhile, learned the skills he would need as defender from his tutor, William of Milemete. William taught Edward the art of war, using his own picture book of the way to wield a sword and ride a horse in armor. He told Edward, "Most noble lord, if you observe these lessons concerning wars and conflict . . . you will enjoy upon earth victory, honor and favor."[93]

Accession to the Throne

The fourteen-year-old Edward's supporters in Parliament soon asserted their influence. On January 7, 1327, they elected him king. Realizing he needed the favor of nobles still loyal to his father, Edward cleverly refused to accept the crown unless he had consent of the old king, who remained imprisoned. The king's resignation sent for and obtained, Edward III's coronation followed on January 24, 1327.

As king, Edward sent Queen Isabella and his guardian, the Earl of Kent, to make peace with the French in a dispute over Guienne, an area in southwestern France. When she gave to her brother, the king of France, the contested lands and Edward agreed to the bargain, it was clear to observers that the real ruler of England was Isabella. Yet if any among the nobles objected to the queen mother's powerful influence over her son, they kept it to themselves. Edward's biographer William Longman writes, "No one dared open his mouth for [either] the good of the King or of the kingdom."[94]

Isabella's lack of loyalty to England's interests was clearer still when the last of her brothers died and there were no more direct male successors to the throne of France. Instead of backing her own son's claim to France's throne, she had Edward swear fealty as vassal to his cousin Philip of Anjou, who became France's king.

To top it all off, she took a lover, Roger Mortimer, the Earl of March, who was sympathetic to Scottish rebels and was clearly defiant of the young king's authority.

A Real King

Despite his apparent deference to his mother, Edward soon took a major step toward assuming his rightful authority. The year after his coronation, on January 24, 1328, he married his choice of a wife, Phillippa of Hainault, a principality in what today is southwestern Belgium. The marriage gave Edward the right to call on Hainault for soldiers.

Early in 1329 Edward made another decisive move. Lawless Scottish militiamen had for some time been raiding English farms and villages along the border. Edward undertook a campaign to drive the raiders out of England and inflict punishment on them for their actions. For three months, Edward and his knights pursued the raiders.

Ultimately, Edward's efforts failed to force the raiders back across the border, despite aid in the form of men from Hainault, and he had to abandon his effort as his men returned to their farms for the autumn harvest. Still, the tall, slender sixteen-year-old cut a fine figure, whether riding horseback in armor or wielding a sword. Celebrating the growing reputation of the strong, agile, and handsome king, the contemporary poet Laurence Minot wrote, "Edward oure cumly [good-looking] king . . . has his woning [winning] with mani cumly knight."[95]

In spite of continuing border troubles, Edward was able to consolidate his power by other means. When his father, the deposed king, died in prison, Edward III garnered the cooperation of a number of Edward II's old supporters. With help from these and other loyalists, he took Roger Mortimer prisoner. Mortimer was charged with murder in connection with the earlier death of the Earl of Kent. Mortimer was convicted, and on November 29, 1330, he was executed. Isabella, deprived of the political support her relationship with Mortimer had provided, was allowed to live, confined to Castle Rising, a stronghold in Norfolk.

Looking Toward France

Though Isabella and Mortimer were out of the picture, Edward still had to rule a country in which nobles were fighting each other for power and the law was poorly enforced. As historian Anthony Verduyn comments, "Edward III inherited the criminals that his father could not bring to justice, as well as the realm he could not rule."[96]

Edward's mother Queen Isabella of France used the power she wielded during the early years of the young king's reign to advance French interests above those of England.

From 1331 to 1339 Edward strengthened his political base by rewarding his friends and best fighters with titles. He packed Parliament with twenty-nine newly created peers who pushed his policies. James S. Bothwell writes, "[Promotion played] an important part in . . . [developing] peaceful relations between nobles."[97]

The young Edward III established peace in England by quelling conflict among the nobility and by defeating the bands of Scottish raiders that plagued the English border.

Over the course of some fifteen years, Edward also engaged the Scottish raiders in numerous battles. Finally, Scotland submitted to England's domination, although with its right to govern its internal affairs recognized.

Meanwhile, Edward became increasingly aggressive against France's King Philip, who had been backing the Scots. Furthermore, Edward believed that he, not Philip, was rightful heir to the throne of France.

The Strategies of War

Edward's claim was rejected by the French. So, with support from Parliament, Edward set out to take the French throne by force. To hire soldiers and build transport ships for an extended war across the English Channel, he levied taxes on England's thriving wool trade. And he was frequently before Parliament, making speeches to justify new arms expenditures.

In 1338 and 1339 Edward began his military campaign against the French, employing a strategy he had learned from the Scots. Rather than mounting a single massive invasion, Edward led small raiding parties, called *chevauchées*, across the channel. Shipload after shipload of his mounted troops plundered and destroyed more than one hundred villages in the north of France.

Edward saw to it that the wealth to be gained from such plunder was widely publicized. He put on parades, tournaments, and other celebrations that allowed his knights to show off their newly won riches. He established the Order of the Garter, made it the highest honor to which a knight could rise, and appointed twenty-five select knights to its ranks. This tactic, says military analyst H.J. Hewitt, proved another of his old teacher's principles of war—that "the prospect of treasure helped to maintain cheerfulness."[98]

The Great Victory at Crécy

Edward's raids wore down his enemy, opening up an opportunity to strike a heavier blow. Eyewitness Jean Froissart explains what happened when the French army, reinforced by Italian mercenaries but tired from a long march, advanced on Edward's rested and well-positioned force:

> The English . . . drawn up in three divisions, and seated on the ground, on seeing their enemies advance, rose up undauntedly and fell into their ranks. . . . There were about 15,000 Genoese crossbow men; but they were quite fatigued, having marched on foot that day six leagues

[about twenty miles], completely armed and carrying their crossbows. . . . The sun shone very bright; but the French had it in their faces, and the English on their backs. When the Genoese were somewhat in order, advancing with their crossbows presented, [they] began to shoot. The English archers then advanced one step forward, and shot their arrows with such force and quickness, that it seemed as if it snowed. When the Genoese felt these arrows, which pierced through their armor, some of them cut the strings of their crossbows, others flung them to the ground, and all turned about and retreated.[99]

Edward's defeat of the French on August 26, 1346, in what came to be known as the Battle of Crécy, was a personal victory. It also brought the English together as a nation. D.A.L. Morgan writes, "[The Battle of Crécy] gave to [the war with France] a mingled character of a dynastic quarrel stemming from and hinging on the person and personal activism of the King, and also a common cause of the political community as a whole; such that, when success did come, it was felt as a more than merely personal achievement."[100]

The Capture of Calais

Edward realized that in order to move beyond this victory to become king of France, he would need to secure his supply lines, and that meant taking over a French port. The target he chose was Calais, just thirty miles across the English Channel from Dover. He laid siege to Calais only after an eleven-month raiding campaign and many attempts to force Philip into a decisive battle. King Philip, on his part, knew that such a battle was not in his interest. He hoped that if he avoided a major fight long enough, eventually the English would give up. In a letter to Parliament Edward expressed his frustration with the French tactics:

Our cousin Philip . . . swore every day that we should not stay a day in France without his giving us battle and we waited from Monday to Sunday, but . . . on Monday morning there came a messenger from the King of France saying that he would place himself where he was not protected by wood, marsh, or water, and that he would give battle to the King of England on the next Thursday. . . . The next day we went towards Flamangrie and staid there all Friday. In the evening three spies were taken, who said that Philip was a league and a half [about five miles] from us and would fight on Saturday. On Saturday we were

74

This illustration depicts the Battle of Crécy in 1346, in which the French were defeated. French archers armed with crossbows (left) proved no match for English longbowmen (right).

ready before day-break, and took some of his spies, who told us that his avant garde was on the field. . . . [We] went to Davenneis, a league and a half from our cousin, and told him we would wait there all Sunday. We found that he had been in such haste to take up a stronger position, that 1,000 of his horsemen had sunk in a marsh. On Monday we heard that the French had [once more] retreated.[101]

Eventually, however, Calais ran out of food and surrendered. The city became a strong English outpost. The conquest of Calais also enhanced Edward's popularity at home. Biographer W. Warburton writes, "Edward saw himself at the commencement of the third decade of his reign at the height of earthly prosperity."[102]

Edward's Heir

Edward signed a truce with Philip and then returned to England in October 1347. Peace was short-lived. In August 1350 the French king died, a victim of the Black Plague epidemic. France's new monarch, Philip's son John, broke the truce, mounting raids far from Calais, into Guienne. Discontinuing the campaign in northern France, Edward sent reinforcements to his son Prince Edward in Bordeaux, the chief English stronghold in Guienne. Prince Edward then set about raiding villages loyal to the French king from Toulouse in southwestern France to Anjou in the northwest.

Finally, the French king himself came to Guienne to give battle. The fight turned against John and his knights near Poitiers, close to Guienne's northern boundary. On September 19, 1356, King John was taken prisoner and held for ransom.

King Edward's wife Philippa begs him to show mercy on the people of Calais. The port city surrendered after running out of food in 1347.

The March on Rheims

With King John a captive and France too poor to pay his ransom, Edward III determined that at last he could claim the throne of France. "Now was the time," says Clifford J. Rogers in *War Cruel and Sharp*, "for the *coup de grâce*: the capture of Rheims, where French kings had for centuries been anointed and crowned, followed by the re-coronation of Edward III as King of France and the subsequent occupation of Paris. Preparations for this massive effort continued through the winter of 1358–59."[103]

In the end, neither side achieved a complete victory. Edward's expedition to Rheims lasted seven months. Rogers writes, "The force gathered for the expedition was . . . the best equipped army Edward had ever assembled."[104] The problem was that France's impoverishment was so extreme that the invaders, hoping to gather food as they went, could not feed themselves adequately. Weakened by hunger, Edward's forces were unable to take any large cities.

At this point, France could not hope to win outright either. Rogers reports, "In order to fend off the further devastation of his kingdom and the very real risk that he might lose it entirely to Edward III, King John pressed his adversary to reopen the peace talks."[105] Edward and John signed the Treaty of Brétigny on November 3, 1360. John remained king of France, and Edward continued to hold Guienne, with England's territory considerably enlarged.

The English did not seem to mind that Edward had failed in his effort to gain the throne of France. The war had strained England's economy and caused a return to Edward's old domestic problems—rampant crime. The English, therefore, were glad to be at rest from war with France.

As he passed his fortieth anniversary on the throne, Edward III returned his attention to reduction of crime. He instituted closer royal supervision of the justices of the peace, making them more accountable in their handling of complaints against thieves and murderers.

Hopes for Edward's Successor

In the late 1360s Edward III was nearing sixty years of age. An old man by medieval standards, he now entered into an agreement that went against the counsel of Parliament. When King Pedro came from Spain to plead for Prince Edward to restore him to his throne, which had been usurped by his illegitimate half brother, King Edward agreed. After all, Pedro promised to reimburse all expenses, and Prince Edward, although he was in poor health, was a great warrior. So Edward saw glory for his heir and little risk for England in undertaking the venture.

King John of France (left) engages Prince Edward in battle at Poitiers in 1356. Prince Edward emerged victorious, and he took John prisoner to hold for ransom.

The Spanish venture proved disastrous. Although Prince Edward won a brilliant victory south of the Pyrenees on April 3, 1368, Pedro made him wait for his pay. While he waited, the heir to England's throne fell ill. Eventually he returned home empty-handed.

Then, in 1369, Edward's beloved Queen Philippa died. In his grief, Edward turned for comfort to a mistress, Alice Perrers. She used her access to the king's chamber to steal the royal jewels. The old man's failure to deal with the theft aroused anger in Parliament and among Edward's children.

The Spanish venture dealt its final blow on June 8, 1376. After suffering as an invalid for years, Prince Edward died. Historian Michael Bennet summarizes Edward's sense of loss: "The death of the Prince of Wales [was] a major blow at both a political and a personal level. [And it] raised a real issue with respect to the succession."[106]

Edward's Last Years

The downturn in the king's fortunes continued when France took advantage of Edward's waning vitality by reconquering large parts of Guienne. Edward did not respond. It seemed that his reign would end poorly.

Nevertheless, Edward III's last months left him one of England's most renowned kings. His sixty-fourth birthday on November 13, 1376, and his golden jubilee as king two months later, on January 17, 1377, were celebrated with great pomp and ceremony. In his retreat in Havering-atte-Bower, he wrote his will. He formally made known his wishes that the throne should go to his grandson, Prince Edward's nine-year-old son, Richard of Bordeaux.

Edward III's health declined rapidly after his jubilee, and he died on June 21, 1377. The oration read at his funeral called Edward both the rudder and the mast of the ship of state: "The rothur [rudder] was nouther ok [oak] ne elm—Hit was Edward the thridde [third], the noble knight . . . bi the rode [cross]! I likne hem to the schipes [ship's] mast."[107]

His Greatest Legacy

Edward's lasting reputation as a warrior is borne out by the fact that the Hundred Years' War, as it came to be called, was without precedent in its destructiveness. Yet Edward's willingness to consult with Parliament advanced England's movement toward advisory government. This was Edward's greatest legacy, says biographer W.M Ormrod: "[His reign] established a new constitutional and moral authority for the [English] monarchy based on the principle of consensual government."[108]

CHAPTER 7

Charles VII: Threat and Turnaround

Charles VII, who took over the kingdom of France as a cynical and doubting young adult, was hardly the sort of whom greatness might have been expected. Opportunistic by nature, he made decisions according to the power and personal advantage that was to be gained. Yet thanks to his talent as an effective financier and administrator, his reign is considered by historians a successful one during which the English finally gave up the Hundred Years' War and French power was greatly enhanced.

At the Center of Intrigues

Charles VII was the eleventh child of King Charles VI of France and Isabella of Bavaria. Born on February 22, 1403, about ten years after his father began to suffer bouts of mental illness, he was the center of the intrigues of his extended family.

At the time of Charles's birth, conflicts among the family-ruled provinces of Anjou, Maine, Burgundy, and Armagnac were intensified by divisions among them over defeating Henry V of England as he extended the so-called Hundred Years' War for the throne of France. The Burgundian branch of the family, in particular, collaborated with the English, while the Armagnac branch resisted them.

In such a political climate death and betrayal were rampant. Louis of Orléans, an uncle of Charles's, was assassinated in 1407 by a kinsman from Burgundy. Two of his brothers died before he was a teenager. Although these deaths put Charles first in line to inherit the throne, his claim was cast in doubt when his mother suggested that he was not the king's son.

The year 1415, when Charles was twelve, was an especially confusing time for the youth, with Henry V's supporters plotting to get rid of every possible heir to France's throne. Early in the year his parents betrothed him to Marie of Anjou in the hope that an alliance with that province would strengthen their cause in the north. But in August and September, Henry's invasions subdued Normandy, and on October 15, 1415, with the help of Charles's Burgundian cousin John the Fearless, Henry won the Battle of Agincourt, bringing the conflict thirty miles closer to Paris.

John's treachery ended in 1419, with Charles witnessing his assassination. The exact circumstances remain mysterious, but historian Albert Guérard, in *France: A Modern History*, suggests that a deadly conspiracy took an unexpected victim: "A meeting was arranged with [Charles] at Montereau. It was hinted—and it is perfectly possible—that John meant to capture the young prince, but it was he who was murdered."[109] With John's death and no further family as his rivals for the throne, Charles, at fourteen, was the only living heir of Charles VI.

Charles VII became king of France at the age of seventeen. The young king's immediate concern was to drive the English out of France.

Leader of the Resistance

The dauphin, as the heir to the French throne was known, was in constant danger. With his father ever more frequently suffering episodes of mental illness, he had few supporters and even fewer reasons to trust anyone. Even with John the Fearless dead, Burgundian collaborators helped the English capture Paris, forcing Charles to flee to Bourges, a small city about two hundred miles to the south.

In Bourges, Charles assumed the title of lieutenant general in the service of his father, a title emptied of its meaning when Charles VI surrendered to the English in 1420. Upon the signing of the Treaty of Troyes, and according to its terms, Henry V married Catherine of Valois, Charles's sister. Now Charles was disinherited as his new brother-in-law had a legal claim to the French throne.

A King Besieged

As it happened, Charles inherited the throne despite the treaty. During the next year two important events completely changed his situation. On May 22, 1421, as lieutenant general, Charles won the Battle of Baugé, and on August 31, Henry V died. Then, just over a year later Charles VI died, on October 21, 1422.

The young Charles VII had taken heart from the Battle of Baugé. As a sign of his coming of age as king, he had married Marie of Anjou. She bore his son, Louis, on July 23, 1423. Immediately after the birth, Charles went to battle again, hoping to force the English out of France. His hopes went unfulfilled. The English defeated him at Cravant on July 31, 1423, and again at Verneuil on August 17, 1424.

These two defeats left Charles badly shaken, once again filled with self-doubt and mistrust. Unable to expel the English and under continuing threats from relatives divided in their loyalties, he narrowly escaped several plots against his life. Barely in control of his tiny island of power in Bourges, he seriously questioned his legitimacy as France's monarch.

Another Turn for the Better

Charles's self-doubt was worsened by his sense that he lacked God's favor. Helplessly headquartered in Bourges—his capital, Paris, held by the hostile Burgundians—King Charles VII could not believe God was blessing his reign. Desperate and unable to discern which faction would best support him, his government at the point of collapse, he held on to the loyalty of a few courtiers and prayed to know if he ought to be king.

The young Charles holds audience with a Dominican friar. During the early years of his reign, Charles VII was constantly threatened by rival claimants to the throne.

The answer to Charles's prayer seemed to come in May 1428. One day a shepherd girl from the borderlands of Burgundy, who became known as Joan of Arc, came to his court claiming that in a vision the saints had told her how to expel the English from France. Seeming to know how Charles had prayed for guidance, she insisted he was the right king for France and that she would recapture Orléans, the town that had been in enemy hands ever since his uncle was assassinated in 1407.

Charles, still mistrusting which warring faction he should choose, followed his religious impulse and put Joan in charge of some troops. Dressed in a knight's armor, she led French troops in a fierce battle that regained Orléans. Historian Guérard writes that the victory raised Charles in the estimation of his religious countrymen: "Joan imparted mystic prestige to the cause of that sorry

In this painting, Joan of Arc stands in full armor with the banner of France at Charles VII's coronation ceremony in the cathedral of Rheims on July 17, 1429.

personage Charles VII. She made him one in the spirit of Christian France with [past rulers] Clovis, Charlemagne, St. Louis."[110]

The Restoration of the Government

Following the capture of Orléans, Charles briefly let go of his doubt. At Joan's insistence, he finally was crowned. The coronation and anointing took place in the cathedral of Rheims in the presence of thirty-six bishops on July 17, 1429.

Although his reign had now clearly received the church's blessing, Charles nevertheless recognized the provisional nature of his support. When Joan wanted to attempt regaining Paris, Charles put her off, wondering if such a move was really in his best interests. Biographer Victoria Mary Sackville-West, suggesting that Paris might have been taken if he had not hesitated, writes, "So uncompromising an alternative could scarcely commend itself to the timorous and wavering soul of Charles VII."[111]

Charles's reluctance worked against him. The Burgundians regrouped and held Paris. They captured Joan and held her for ransom, further discrediting her by charging her with witchcraft and heresy, charges that, if she were convicted, would incur the sentence of burning at the stake. Charles was in a corner. He clearly owed a great debt to her. But he had just been crowned in the presence of thirty-six bishops. He resolved the dilemma by doing nothing. Feeling he could not afford to support a heretic, he let her burn. Biographer Mary Gordon writes, "However inspired Charles may have been by Joan's presence, he was not going to [go ahead] without the support of the church."[112]

In the wake of Joan's execution, Charles made it his priority to convince the Burgundians to forsake the English cause and support the French crown. In the end, money bought Burgundy's cooperation. According to the terms reached at the Congress of Arras in 1435. Charles paid the Burgundians four hundred thousand gold coins and gave up control of several towns. Biographer Philippe Bully notes his belief that Charles really had no choice but to buy off his opponents: "[Charles, seeing advantages ahead] let that be: at the moment, there was no other possibility."[113]

Sackville-West takes a harsher stance, suggesting that Charles's treatment of Joan of Arc shows him to be less than courageous:

> Charles, although he could run all risks for objects where his heart was really engaged, and could bribe the duke of Burgundy with Compiégne as part of an unnecessary and foolish truce, lay low, small, mean, and evasive as he always was, when it came to the point of ransoming the most valuable prisoner in his kingdom. He left his best friend to her fate.[114]

The Return to Paris

Thanks to the deal he had struck with the Burgundians, Charles was able, at last, to return to Paris. His return to the capital enhanced his legitimacy as leader of France. Charles, however, failed to follow up on his advantage. Instead of using his newly consolidated power to build further popularity, he spent his time in high living that

Charles VII parades through Paris during a lavish celebration of his return to the capital. Such sumptuous pageantry contrasted sharply with poverty among the common people.

contrasted strongly with the poverty of the commoners. Biographer Thomas Basin writes, "[The king] was steeping himself in banquets and pleasures, languishing in debauchery, luxury and slothful idleness, displaying not the slightest concern [for his] subjects."[115]

Poverty and insecurity were ruining the nation. In the late 1430s, especially in Normandy, people could hardly make a living. Roving bands of freebooters called *écorcheurs* ("scorchers"), were raiding farms and villages.

In 1440 led by Charles's own son Louis, the peasants rebelled against these conditions and were ready to take over Paris and the government. Historian Mark Spencer writes, "Alerted to the plot, Charles VII took uncharacteristically decisive action."[116] Charles put down the rebellion with a combination of force and bribery and exiled his son to Burgundy.

Over the next ten years Charles's forces reconquered Normandy. By 1450 his hold on a more unified country was well established, to the point that he felt he could offer the rebels amnesty. Malcolm G.A. Vale quotes his edict: "[The king wishes] to keep and to hold good peace and union between our subjects, without their having reason to remember, one against the other, the evils and troubles done and perpetrated during the wars and conflicts which have taken place within our kingdom."[117]

Reform of the Army

The Normandy campaign, which relied on mercenaries, showed Charles the weakness of having to hire soldiers from wherever he could get them. Even before the end of the rebellion, Charles had instituted a far-reaching reform of his armed forces. He first reformed army discipline by giving the troops regular pay and by purchasing their armor and weapons for them, using funds from his own treasury. He then instituted a system of standardized groupings of men, called lances, and supported them in assigned garrisons. This meant that soldiers no longer had to roam through the country looking for food. Finally, he reserved for himself the right to call up troops.

Charles's reform of the military began the transformation of France into a nation rather than a feudal state. It did this in two ways: First, since Charles himself was the only one who could call up troops, he became responsible for protecting the nobles. This increased the number of nobles who stayed at the royal court to gain his favor. Second, the nobles' power was reduced. The loss of their personal military retinues greatly limited their direct influence over the affairs of their provinces.

Financier and Overseer

The reform of the army, however, was a great drain on Charles's personal treasury. Faced with the constant need to pay for the upkeep of his army, Charles became a financial administrator. His interest in improving the army gave him insights into how to collect money. He appointed administrators of his finances and spent regular hours going over the books with them. He punished tax delinquents by confiscating their property. Guérard writes, "The King ceased at last to be a mere feudal lord and had the means to pursue a royal policy."[118]

Charles's financial needs continued to be driven, in part, by his high living. More than ever, he indulged his love of handsome furniture, fine clothes, and the newest in exotic seasonings, such as mustard from the town of Dijon. The novelist Alexandre Dumas writes, "Historical figures who favored mustard included Charles VII."[119] Also, for several years, Charles's love of luxury included a court mistress, the beautiful Agnes Sorel, until her death in February 1450.

Furthermore, what Charles considered reform did not meet with the approval of all Frenchmen. In the opinion of the contemporary critic of Charles's reign, Thomas Basin, the army represented the worst of Charles's self-serving administration. He writes, "The gravest sins of Charles VII lay in the standing mercenary army, the heavy taxes which sustained it, and the corruption that flourished in the wake of both."[120]

The Capture of Bordeaux

From 1449 to 1461, Charles mostly left it up to his army to keep peace along the borders of Gascony, where English sympathizers remained strong. Leading an army into battle became less and less a way Charles wanted to spend his time. Biographer Malcolm G.A. Vale comments, "It can be surmised that the active waging of war was not to his taste. He was . . . not bellicose [warlike] by nature. His talents lay rather in the council, and the counting-house."[121]

Nevertheless, Charles experienced success in Gascony. A well-disciplined army paid off for him as he received surrender after surrender throughout the region. The story of the town of Cadillac, reported by Vale, is an example of Charles's reception: "On his arrival, they surrendered. The captain was executed on his orders. His sovereignty was no longer to be mocked."[122]

On October 19, 1453, Charles returned to Bordeaux, which his forces had earlier besieged, to receive the surrender of the English forces holding the city. Historian Richard Cavendish writes that the capture of Bordeaux ended a costly chapter in France's history: "When Bordeaux surrendered, this marked the conventionally accepted end of the [Hundred Years'] War, [a war] fought entirely on French soil and thought to have reduced the population of France by perhaps half."[123]

No More Soldiering

The king did not go to battle again. Between his entertainments and his increasingly frail health, Charles looked more and more for ways to make administration easier. He delegated all duties but his financial oversight. However, always looking for ways to project and enhance his royal influence, and recognizing the potential offered by the recently developed printing press he sent delegates to Germany to talk to Johannes Gutenberg, its inventor.

The obvious reason for Charles's withdrawal from much of the active administration of his kingdom was the fact that he was often in great pain. His malady, said by some to be syphilis, caused a running ulcer of the leg and ulcers of the mouth. Removal of a diseased tooth appears to have been extremely painful. "An abscess seems to have formed on the gums," writes Vale. "Accom-

In the later years of his reign, Charles suffered from a number of physical ailments. His poor health forced him to delegate most of his administrative duties.

panied, as it probably was, by acute inflammation of the mouth and of the upper digestive tract, any form of feeding would have been intolerably painful."[124]

Pain, Paranoia, and Repentance

The pain Charles suffered seems to have made him somewhat paranoid. His long-standing mistrust of others became concentrated upon his son Louis, still residing in the Burgundian court. The result was that Charles and his son remained at odds. Biographer Michel Hérubel writes, "Charles was the unifier, that is to say, with his enemy. . . . His son was not brought back."[125]

Near death, Charles recaptured his religious spirit. On July 22, 1461, realizing that he was dying, Charles prayed aloud for forgiveness, invoking Saint Mary Magdalene, whom the church honored on this day: "I praise my God and the mercy he grants me,

This illustration depicts King Charles VII on his deathbed in 1461. Charles is best remembered as the king who drove the English from France.

that the greatest sinner in the world dies on the feast of the repentant sinner."[126] Charles VII died at the age of fifty-eight, in the thirty-ninth year of his reign. An imposing funeral cortege preceded him to his burial place in St. Denis.

A Marvelous Legacy

Charles's legacy was his restoration of France to the French. To the advantage of his son, King Louis XI, Charles left a centralized government largely independent of influence by the church as well as concern for public opinion. Louis soon pushed his advantage, some said to the point of tyranny. In a new era of exploration and world travel, his sovereign power flourished, signaling the virtual end of the Middle Ages. In contrast to what Charles VII had inherited, says Philippe Bully, his legacy was no less than marvelous: "Order was reestablished, the great nobles were no longer fighting, French authority was reaffirmed over the English, the army was reorganized, enemies were expelled from the land, and prosperity was restored."[127]

NOTES

Chapter 1: Charlemagne: Making Empire Holy

1. Quoted in M.J. Swanton, trans. and ed., *The Anglo-Saxon Chronicle*. New York: Routledge, 1996, p. 51.

2. François Louis Ganscholf, *Frankish Institutions Under Charlemagne*, trans. Roger and Mary Lyon. Providence, RI: Brown University Press, 1968, p. 9.

3. Maurice Keen, *A History of Medieval Europe*. New York: Frederick A. Praeger, 1967, p. 20.

4. Keen, *A History of Medieval Europe*, pp. 34–35.

5. Ganscholf, *Frankish Institutions Under Charlemagne*, p. 10.

6. Quoted in Swanton, *The Anglo-Saxon Chronicle*, p. 53.

7. Allen Cabaniss, *Charlemagne*. New York: Twayne, 1972, p. 26.

8. Robert Folz, *The Coronation of Charlemagne, 25 December 800*, trans. J.E. Anderson. London: Routledge & Kegan Paul, 1974, p. 36.

9. Folz, *The Coronation of Charlemagne*, p. 49.

10. Quoted in Folz, *The Coronation of Charlemagne*, p. 99.

11. Einhard, *Vita Karoli Magni: The Life of Charlemagne*, trans. Evelyn Scherabon Firchow and Edwin H. Zeydel. Coral Gables, FL: University of Miami Press, 1972, p. 97.

12. Einhard, *Vita Karoli Magni*, pp. 69–71.

13. Einhard, *Vita Karoli Magni*, p. 97.

14. Folz, *The Coronation of Charlemagne*, p. 135.

15. Folz, *The Coronation of Charlemagne*, p. 140.

16. Donald A. Bullough, *The Age of Charlemagne*. New York: G.P. Putnam's Sons, 1966, p. 174.

17. Einhard, *Vita Karoli Magni*, p. 87.

18. Einhard, *Vita Karoli Magni*, p. 105.

19. Quoted in Bullough, *The Age of Charlemagne*, p. 198.

20. Cabaniss, *Charlemagne*, p. 141.

Chapter 2: William the Conqueror: Holding on to Power

21. David Armine Howarth, *1066: The Year of the Conquest*. New York: Dorset, 1978, p. 64.

22. Kenneth M. Setton, "900 Years Ago: The Norman Conquest," *National Geographic*, August 1966, p. 206.
23. Howarth, *1066*, p. 66.
24. Howarth, *1066*, p. 73.
25. Howarth, *1066*, p. 95.
26. Elisabeth van Houts, "The Norman Conquest Through European Eyes," *English Historical Review*, September 1995, p. 832.
27. Setton, "900 Years Ago," p. 231.
28. Quoted in Maurice Ashley, *The Life and Times of William I*. New York: Cross River, 1992, p. 45.
29. Quoted in Setton, "900 Years Ago," p. 247.
30. Quoted in Ashley, *The Life and Times of William I*, p. 207.
31. Ashley, *The Life and Times of William I*, p. 18.
32. Setton, "900 Years Ago," p. 206.
33. Thomas B. Costain, *The Conquerors*. New York: Doubleday, 1949, pp. 25–26.
34. Costain, *The Conquerors*, p. 26.
35. Quoted in Ashley, *The Life and Times of William I*, p. 216.
36. Costain, *The Conquerors*, p. 398.

Chapter 3: Frederick Barbarossa: Imperial Justice

37. Marcel Pacaut, *Frederick Barbarossa*, trans. A.J. Pomerans. New York: Charles Scribner's Sons, 1970, p. 47.
38. Pacaut, *Frederick Barbarossa*, p. 48.
39. Otto of Freising, *The Deeds of Frederick Barbarossa*, trans. Charles Christopher Mierow with the collaboration of Richard Emery. New York: W.W. Norton, 1996, p. 116.
40. Quoted in Otto, *The Deeds of Frederick Barbarossa*, pp. 331–32.
41. Quoted in Otto, *The Deeds of Frederick Barbarossa*, p. 189.
42. Quoted in Thomas Carson, ed. and trans., *Barbarossa in Italy*. New York: Italica, 1994, p. 52.
43. Otto, *The Deeds of Frederick Barbarossa*, p. 149.
44. Peter Munz, *Frederick Barbarossa: A Study in Medieval Politics,* Ithaca, NY: Cornell University Press, 1969, p. 314.
45. Quoted in Pacaut, *Frederick Barbarossa*, pp. 164–65.
46. Pacaut, *Frederick Barbarossa*, p. 171.
47. Pacaut, *Frederick Barbarossa*, p. 181.
48. Munz, *Frederick Barbarossa*, p. 39.
49. Munz, *Frederick Barbarossa*, p. 396.

50. Pacaut, *Frederick Barbarossa*, p. 208.

Chapter 4: Genghis Khan: Inflexible Conquest

51. Willard Price, "Japan Faces Russia in Manchuria," *National Geographic*, November 1942, p. 625.
52. Leo de Hartog, *Genghis Khan: Conqueror of the World*. New York: Barnes & Noble, 1999, p. 13.
53. De Hartog, *Genghis Khan*, p. 13.
54. De Hartog, *Genghis Khan*, p. 14.
55. Quoted in Urgunge Onon, ed. and trans., *The Secret History of the Mongols*. Richmond, UK: Curzon, 2001, p. 247.
56. Quoted in Onon, *The Secret History of the Mongols*, p. 81.
57. *Economist*, "The Canonization of Genghis," February 10, 1990, p. 95.
58. Quoted in Onon, *The Secret History of the Mongols*, pp. 100–101.
59. Quoted in Alexander O. Victor, introduction to *The Vinland Map and the Tartar Relation*, by R.A. Skelton, Thomas E. Marston, and George D. Painter. New Haven, CT: Yale University Press, 1965, p. 29.
60. Quoted in Onon, *The Secret History of the Mongols*, p. 190.
61. Adam T. Kessler, "Genghis Khan: Treasures from Inner Mongolia," *USA Today*, May 1994, p. 52.
62. J.H. Liddell Hart, *Great Captains Unveiled*. New York: Da Capo, 1996, p. 8.
63. Kessler, "Genghis Khan," p. 55.
64. Hart, *Great Captains Unveiled*, p. 8.
65. Hart, *Great Captains Unveiled*, pp. 16–17.
66. Quoted in Onon, *The Secret History of the Mongols*, p. 252.
67. De Hartog, *Genghis Khan*, p. 135.
68. Kessler, "Genghis Khan," p. 53.
69. De Hartog, *Genghis Khan*, pp. 16–17.

Chapter 5: Louis IX: The Idealistic Monarch

70. Marion A. Habig, *The Franciscan Book of Saints*. Chicago: Franciscan Herald, 1959, p. 602.
71. Daniel Borzeix, René Pautal, and Jacques Servat, *Louis IX et l'Occitainie*. Nîmes, France: Cap e Cap, 1976, p. 58. Author's translation.
72. Régine Pernoud, *Blanche of Castile*, trans. Henry Noel. New York: Coward, McCann & Geoghegan, 1975, p. 178.

73. Quoted in Winifred F. Knox, *The Court of a Saint*. London: Methuen, 1909, p. 120.

74. Quoted in Habig, *The Franciscan Book of Saints*, p. 608.

75. Quoted in Jean de Joinville, "The Life of Saint Louis," in Jean de Joinville and Geoffroi de Villehardouin, *Chronicles of the Crusades*, trans. Margaret R.B. Shaw. New York: Penguin, 1980, p. 321.

76. Quoted in Joinville, "The Life of Saint Louis," pp. 322–23.

77. Habig, *The Franciscan Book of Saints*, p. 606.

78. Quoted in Knox, *The Court of a Saint*, p. 130.

79. Knox, *The Court of a Saint*, pp. 120–21.

80. Simon Lloyd, "The Crusades of St. Louis," *History Today*, May 1997, p. 41.

81. Joinville, "The Life of Saint Louis," p. 331.

82. Albert Guérard, *France: A Modern History*. Ann Arbor: University of Michigan Press, 1959.

83. Knox, *The Court of a Saint*, p. 220.

84. Quoted in Knox, *The Court of a Saint*, p. 224.

85. Margaret Wade Labarge, *Saint Louis: Louis IX, Most Christian King of France*. Boston: Little, Brown, 1968, p. 45.

86. Borzeix, Pautal, and Servat, *Louis IX et l'Occitainie*, p. 93.

87. Quoted in Keen, *A History of Medieval Europe*, p. 157.

88. Quoted in Keen, *A History of Medieval Europe*, p. 344.

89. Knox, *The Court of a Saint*, p. 346.

90. Quoted in Guérard, *France*, p. 92.

91. Lloyd, "The Crusades of St. Louis," p. 37.

92. Quoted in Joinville, "The Life of Saint Louis," p. 348.

Chapter 6: Edward III: Princely and Popular

93. Quoted in D.A.L. Morgan, "The Political After-Life of Edward III: The Apotheosis of a Warmonger," *English Historical Review*, September 1997, p. 858.

94. William Longman, *The History of the Life and Times of Edward the Third*, vol. 1. New York: Burt Franklin, 1969, pp. 9–10.

95. Quoted in Thomas H. Ohlgren, "Edwardus Redivivus in a Gest of Robyn Hode," *Journal of English and Germanic Philology*, January 2000, p. 1.

96. Anthony Verduyn, "The Politics of Law and Order During the Early Years of Edward III," *English Historical Review*, October 1993, p. 842.

97. James S. Bothwell, "'Escheat with Heir': Guardianship, Upward Mobility, and Political Reconciliation in the Reign of Edward III," *Canadian Journal of History*, August 2000, p. 241.

98. H.J. Hewitt, *The Organization of War Under Edward III, 1338–62*. New York: Barnes & Noble, 1966, p. 105.

99. Jean Froissart, "The Chronicles of Froissart," in *Chronicle and Romance: Froissart, Malory, Holinshed*. New York: P.F. Colliers, 1910, pp. 42–43.

100. Morgan, "The Political After-Life of Edward III," p. 858.

101. Quoted in Longman, *The History of the Life and Times of Edward the Third*, vol. 1, pp. 153–55.

102. W. Warburton, *Edward III*. New York: Charles Scribner's Sons, 1892, p. 135.

103. Clifford J. Rogers, *War Cruel and Sharp: English Strategy Under Edward III, 1327–1360*. Woodbridge, UK: Boydell, 2000, p. 397.

104. Rogers, *War Cruel and Sharp*, p. 398.

105. Rogers, *War Cruel and Sharp*, p. 397.

106. Michael Bennett, "Edward III's Entail and the Succession to the Crown," *English Historical Review*, June 1998, p. 581.

107. Quoted in Ohlgren, "Edwardus Redivivus," p. 1.

108. W.M. Ormrod, "Edward III: The Career of the King," *History Today*, June 2002, p. 20.

Chapter 7: Charles VII: Threat and Turnaround

109. Guérard, *France*, p. 108.

110. Guérard, *France*, p. 109.

111. Victoria Mary Sackville-West, *Saint Joan of Arc*. New York: Literary Guild, 1936, p. 202.

112. Mary Gordon, *Joan of Arc*. Auckland, New Zealand: Viking Penguin, 2000, p. 43.

113. Philippe Bully, *Charles VII: Le "Roi des Merveilles."* Paris: Tallandier, 1994, p. 223. Author's translation.

114. Sackville-West, *Saint Joan of Arc*, p. 266.

115. Quoted in Mark Spencer, *Thomas Basin (1412–1490): The History of Charles VII and Louis XI*. Nieuwkoop, Netherlands: De Graaf, 1997, p. 105.

116. Spencer, *Thomas Basin*, p. 106.

117. Quoted in Malcolm G.A. Vale, *Charles VII*. Berkeley and Los Angeles: University of California Press, 1974, p. 153.

118. Guérard, *France*, p. 113.
119. Quoted in *Antaeus*, "Mustard: Not for Bread Alone," Spring 1992, p. 131.
120. Quoted in Spencer, *Thomas Basin*, p. 133.
121. Vale, *Charles VII*, p. 141.
122. Vale, *Charles VII*, p. 140.
123. Richard Cavendish, "The End of the Hundred Years' War, October 19th, 1453," *History Today*, October 2003, p. 57.
124. Vale, *Charles VII*, p. 189.
125. Michael Hérubel, *Charles VII*. Paris: Olivier Orban, 1981, p. 363.
126. Quoted in Hérubel, "*Charles VII*, p. 371. Author's translation.
127. Bully, *Charles VII*, p. ii. Author's translation.

FOR FURTHER READING

Karen Armstrong, *Holy War: The Crusades and Their Impact on Today's World.* New York: Scribner, 1982. Insights on how the rulers of the Middle Ages have affected our lives today.

Susan Banfield, *Charlemagne.* New York: Chelsea House, 1986. This biography of the first emperor of the Holy Roman Empire emphasizes his personality and accomplishments. Largely contemporary illustrations.

Polly Schoyer Brooks and Nancy Zinsser Walworth, *The World of Walls: The Middle Ages in Western Europe.* Philadelphia: J.B. Lippincott, 1966. A collective biography with brief overviews, excerpts from Chaucer and *The Song of Roland*, historical art, but very sparse documentation.

Trevor Cairns, *The Middle Ages.* Minneapolis: Lerner, 1975. This is a remarkably clear and comprehensive study of the times, people, institutions, and events from 1100 to 1500, with maps, illustrations, time lines, and many other study features.

Cherese Cartlidge, *The Crusades: Failed Holy Wars.* San Diego: Lucent Books, 2002. A thematic presentation of the movements, circumstances, politics, and people who waged war in the name of religion.

Geoffrey Chaucer, *Canterbury Tales.* Ed. and trans. Barbara Cohen. New York: Lothrop, Lee & Shepard, 1988. Four of Chaucer's Canterbury tales made wonderfully accessible.

Susan Churchill, *Castles.* New York: Barnes & Noble, 1998. Beautifully illustrated and furnished with accompanying activity kit and poster, this well-researched book provides a complete picture of life in the castles of the High Middle Ages.

Sneed B. Collard III, *1,000 Years Ago on Planet Earth.* Boston: Houghton Mifflin, 1999. Spare text, maps, and one illustration for each continent and several individual countries, presenting them as they were at the beginning of the second millennium.

Mike Corbishley, *The Middle Ages.* New York: Facts On File, 1990. Maps and many meticulously documented illustrations cover cities, the Crusades, lands, castles, churches, and many other aspects of medieval life and events.

James A. Corrick, *Life of a Medieval Knight.* San Diego: Lucent Books, 2001. Provides a comprehensive understanding of warriors in the times of kings such as Louis IX and Edward III.

Imogen Dawson, *Clothes and Crafts in the Middle Ages.* Milwaukee: Gareth Stevens, 1997. Lavishly illustrated from contemporary and early art sources, this presentation of medieval culture is both appealing and helpful in understanding the people and countries of Europe during the 1200s through the 1400s.

P.C. Doherty, *Ghostly Murders*. New York: St. Martin's, 1997. A murder mystery based on the life of Edward III in Chaucer's "The Priest's Tale."

———, *A Tapestry of Murders*. New York: St. Martin's, 1997. A novel based on "The Lawyer's Tale" by Geoffrey Chaucer. Fictionalized characters include Isabella, daughter of Philip IV of France, who became the mother of Edward III.

———, *A Tournament of Murder*. New York: St. Martin's, 1997. A novel based on "The Franklin's Tale" by Chaucer.

Editors of Time-Life Books, *The Age of Calamity: Time Frame* A.D. *1300–1400*. Alexandria, VA: Time-Life, 1996. Covering such topics as the Black Death, the Hundred Years' War, and the incursions into Europe by the Ottoman Turks and the Mongols, or Tartars, these lavishly illustrated essays concentrate on an overall picture.

———, *Fury of the Northmen*. Alexandria, VA: Time-Life, 1988. This book covers the time between Charlemagne and William the Conqueror.

———, *The March of Islam*. Alexandria, VA: Time-Life, 1988. This work provides background for understanding Europe's response to Muslim invasions.

Michael Gibson, *The Vikings*. Morristown, NJ: Silver Burdett, 1976. Well researched from ancient and modern sources, this beautifully illustrated history and cultural exposition provides excellent background for medieval study.

Miriam Greenblatt, *Genghis Khan and the Mongol Empire*. New York: Marshall Cavendish, 2002. A two-part account, consisting of a short biography of Genghis Khan and a cultural study, and also three extended excerpts from Mongolian literature. Illustrated with early Persian art reproductions.

Jeff Hays, ed., *The Middle Ages*. San Diego: Greenhaven, 2002. Many primary and secondary documents collected and arranged in chronological order to help the reader establish relationships among various events across the world scene in medieval times.

Kathryn Hinds, *Life in the Middle Ages: The Church*. New York: Marshall Cavendish, 2001. Hinds's lucid narration of ten aspects of religious life, including some short biographies, concentrates on Europe from 500 to 1500. It contains an excellent reading list and accompanying illustrations but no documentation.

Vicki León, *Outrageous Women of the Middle Ages*. New York: John Wiley, 1982. Maps, sidebars, scholarship, and lively writing make this collective biography interesting, especially with regard to Louis IX's grandmother, Eleanor of Aquitaine. No documentation.

John M. Merriman, ed., *For Want of a Horse: Choice and Chance in History*. Lexington, MA: Stephen Greene, 1982. Selections from a variety of authors explore how choice and chance have shaped history. Pleasantly humorous and challengingly speculative and not, by any means, confined to the Middle Ages.

Kathleen Paparchontis, *100 Leaders Who Changed the World*. Milwaukee: World Almanac Library, 2003. These one-page biographies with a time line from 2500 B.C. to the present, plus suggested projects, can help with historical background.

James Riordan, *Tales of King Arthur*. New York: Rand McNally, 1984. Using several early sources, Riordan translates and adapts the tales of King Arthur in chronological order.

Sheila Sancha, *The Luttrell Village: Country Life in the Middle Ages*. New York: Thomas Y. Crowell, 1982. Meticulously researched from contemporary and archaeological sources, this study of an English village in Lincolnshire provides a modern explanation of drawings made for Sir Geoffrey Luttrell in the early 1300s.

Nigel Saul, ed., *The Oxford Illustrated History of Medieval England*. New York: Oxford University Press, 1997. Provides much helpful detail and background in text, illustrations, and captions.

Philip Arthur Sauvain, *Do You Know? About Castles and Crusaders*. New York: Warwick, 1986. Easy-reading, one-page explanations of fourteen themes, such as trade, monastic life, the Norman Conquest, and Islam make this a good starting place for study of the Middle Ages.

Jeffrey L. Singman, *Daily Life in Medieval Europe*. Westport, CT: Greenwood, 1999. An overview of cultural practices in the Middle Ages.

Robert Taylor, *Life in Genghis Khan's Mongolia*. San Diego: Lucent Books, 2001. Chapters on family life, religion, economics, and militarism, and the influence of Mongolian culture on the conquest of Asia and eastern Europe.

Jay Williams, *Life in the Middle Ages*. New York: Random House, 1966. Williams's grasp of medieval social and cultural life is enhanced by many contemporary illustrations, with careful picture credits. However, captions often do not tell the dates of artwork, and narration is not entirely objective.

Works Consulted

Books

Maurice Ashley, *The Life and Times of William I.* New York: Cross River, 1992. Richly illustrated with scenes from the Bayeux Tapestry and other medieval art and artifacts, this biography of William the Conqueror adds much to an understanding of medieval and modern Europe.

Richard Barber, *Edward, Prince of Wales and Aquitaine: A Biography of the Black Prince.* New York: Charles Scribner's Sons, 1978. Shows the relationship of Edward III with his oldest son and heir to be a shaping influence in the career of this warrior/politician.

Malcolm Billings, *The Cross and the Crescent: A History of the Crusades.* New York: Sterling, 1987. Explores the conflicts between Christendom and Islam.

Daniel Borzeix, René Pautal, and Jacques Servat, *Louis IX et l'Occitainie.* Nîmes, France: Cap e Cap, 1976. A study guide in French with chapters on the places and personages of France in the High Middle Ages.

Donald A. Bullough, *The Age of Charlemagne.* New York: G.P. Putnam's Sons, 1966. This beautifully illustrated study of Charlemagne emphasizes his cultural contributions.

Philippe Bully, *Charles VII: Le "Roi des Merveilles."* Paris: Tallandier, 1994. Bully, writing in French, emphasizes the contrast between the beginning and the end of Charles's reign, particularly citing the good outcomes from the unlikely facets of his character as a person and a king.

Allen Cabaniss, *Charlemagne.* New York: Twayne, 1972. This detailed biography of the king of the Franks provides skilled analysis and sidelights on many other people and events that shaped the early history of the Holy Roman Empire.

John Cadwalader, *King Edward the Third, with the Fall of Mortimer, Earl of March, 1691.* Philadelphia: University of Pennsylvania, 1949. An annotated edition of a play about the intrigues of Mortimer against Edward III.

John Carey, ed., *Eyewitness History.* Cambridge, MA: Harvard University Press, 1988. Several selections written in the Middle Ages are included in this volume of excerpts by well-reputed historians.

Thomas Carson, ed. and trans., *Barbarossa in Italy.* New York: Italica, 1994. A latin poem about Barbarossa's conquest of Italy.

Thomas B. Costain, *The Conquerors*. New York: Doubleday, 1949. A narrative of the Norman period of English history, from William the Conqueror through the signing of the Magna Carta. Many short biographies of little-known leaders and a bibliography of sources, but no specific documentation. Includes maps.

————, *The Three Edwards*. New York: Charles Scribner's Sons, 1958. This collective biography of Edward III and his father and grandfather is descriptive and provides the author's insights into character and relationship but no documentation.

Einhard, *Vita Karoli Magni: The Life of Charlemagne*. Trans. Evelyn Scherabon Firchow and Edwin H. Zeydel. Coral Gables, FL: University of Miami Press, 1972. The Latin text written by Charlemagne's first biographer, who knew the ruler, is printed on pages opposite the translation.

Robert Folz, *The Coronation of Charlemagne, 25 December 800*. Trans. J.E. Anderson. London: Routledge & Kegan Paul, 1974. Mainly an analysis of the rule and style of Charlemagne, along with a detailed analysis of his crowning as emperor.

Jean Froissart, "The Chronicles of Froissart," in *Chronicle and Romance: Froissart, Malory, Holinshed*. New York: P.F. Collier, 1910. Brief excerpts from various histories, translated and collected into one anthology.

François Louis Ganshoff, *Frankish Institutions Under Charlemagne*. Trans. Roger and Mary Lyon. Providence, RI: Brown University Press, 1968. An overview of the inheritance and legacy of Charlemagne.

Marija Gimbutas, *The Slavs*. New York: Praeger, 1971. An archaeological study of early Slavic inhabitants of eastern Europe, whose descendants are known today as Bulgarians, Slovakians, Serbs, Croatians, and Byelorussians.

Ernst Desiré Glasson, *Le Parlement de Paris: Son Role Politique Depuis le Reigne de Charles VII Jusqu'a la Revolution*. Geneva: Slatkins-Megariotes, 1974. Discusses Charles VII's innovations in the governing structures of France, especially in relation to representative government.

Anthony Goodman, *John of Gaunt: The Exercise of Princely Power in Fourteenth-Century Europe*. New York: St. Martin's, 1992. Details of the operations and influence of King Edward III's second-oldest son and his influence on Parliament.

Mary Gordon, *Joan of Arc*. Auckland, New Zealand: Viking Penguin, 2000. Emphasis in this biography is not on Charles VII. Gordon provides many religious details.

Michael Grant, *Dawn of the Middle Ages*. New York: Bonanza, 1981. Cultural studies of the peoples that populated Europe from the rise of the Byzantine Empire to the reign of Charlemagne.

Vivian Green, *The Madness of Kings*. New York: St. Martin's, 1993. A collective biography of several rulers who had mental problems. Includes Charles VI of France and Edward III's grandson Richard II.

Albert Guérard, *France: A Modern History*. Ann Arbor: University of Michigan Press, 1959. Provides much background on the people and events that shaped modern France.

Marion A. Habig, *The Franciscan Book of Saints*. Chicago: Franciscan Herald, 1959. A collection of brief biographies of saints.

Barbara Hanawalt, *The Middle Ages: An Illustrated History*. New York: Oxford University Press, 1998. Provides abundant background information on the Middle Ages, with lots of illustrations.

J.H. Liddell Hart, *Great Captains Unveiled*. New York: Da Capo, 1996. Includes an analysis of Genghis Khan's military ability.

Leo de Hartog, *Genghis Khan: Conqueror of the World*. New York: Barnes & Noble, 1999. A deeply researched biography of the Mongol leader.

Michel Hérubel, *Charles VII*. Paris: Olivier Orban, 1981. Hérubel, writing in French, attends to the development of Charles VII's character as a person, showing how his growth benefited France's statehood.

H.J. Hewitt, *The Organization of War Under Edward III, 1338–62*. New York: Barnes & Noble, 1966. Studies all aspects of Edward III's mobilization of economic and military forces to invade France and Spain and take over Scotland.

Nicholas Hooper and Matthew Bennett, *Cambridge Illustrated Atlas: Warfare in the Middle Ages, 768–1487*. Cambridge: Cambridge University Press, 1996. Provides a history of the major campaigns and battles of western Europe and analyzes means and methods of warfare used and reasons for success and/or failure. Includes colored modern maps as well as extensive illustrations from ancient sources.

David Armine Howarth, *1066: The Year of the Conquest*. New York: Dorset, 1978. An account of William's claim to the English throne, enlivened by emphasis on the personalities of the protagonists, especially of King Harold. Includes maps, an index, and illustrations.

Francis Hueffer, *The Troubadours: A History of Provençal Life and Literature in the Middle Ages*. London: Chatto & Windus, Piccadilly, 1878. Discusses how the poetry of the homeland of Queen Margaret of France influenced the outcome of wars and the trajectories of kingdoms.

J.E.A. Jocliffe, *The Constitutional History of Medieval England from the English Settlement to 1485*. New York: D. Van Nostrand, 1937. Provides important insights into the political process as it developed.

Jean de Joinville, "The Life of Saint Louis," in Jean de Joinville & Geoffroi de Villehardouin, *Chronicles of the Crusades*. Trans. M.R.B. Shaw. New York: Penguin, 1980. A contemporary account of the life of the leader of the Seventh and Eighth Crusades, King Louis IX of France.

Maurice Keen, *A History of Medieval Europe*. New York: Frederick A. Praeger, 1967. Keen's history of the Middle Ages, recounted as a succession of broad sweeps of influence (feudalism, papacy, military campaigns, strong rulers, studies, and religious beliefs), provides a lucid overview of these complex times.

Winifred F. Knox, *The Court of a Saint*. London: Methuen, 1909. A study of how the Capetian line of kings of France and the work of Christendom brought about the triumph of monarchy.

Margaret Wade Labarge, *Saint Louis: Louis IX, Most Christian King of France*. Boston: Little, Brown, 1968. Careful use of contemporary sources makes this biography a rich source of information on both the life of King Louis and on the times in which he lived.

Philip Lindsay and Reg Groves, *The Peasants' Revolt, 1381*. London: Hutchinson, 1950. Includes spirited essays on some aspects of English political and economic life that made the peasants' revolt possible.

William Longman, *The History of the Life and Times of Edward the Third*. Vol. 1. New York: Burt Franklin, 1969. This centenary reprint of Longman's biography provides a nineteenth-century overview of the reign of the king who started the Hundred Years' War.

Robert Marshall, *Storm from the East*. Berkeley and Los Angeles: University of California Press, 1993. Discusses the effects of the invasion of the Mongols.

Shailer Mathews, ed., *Select Medieval Documents and Other Material Illustrating the History of Church and Empire, 754 A.D.–1254 A.D.* New York: Silver Burdett, 1900. Selections taken chiefly from legal documents illustrating the political and economic history of the Carolingians, Saxons, Franconians, and Hohenstaufens.

Peter Munz, *Frederick Barbarossa: A Study in Medieval Politics*. Ithaca, NY: Cornell University Press, 1969. Using an impressive number of sources, Munz explains the importance of Frederick's reign. Illustrated with several likenesses of the emperor.

Urgunge Onon, ed. and trans., *The Secret History of the Mongols*. Richmond, UK: Curzon, 2001. Authentic translation and interpretation of the chief resource available for studying the Mongol Empire by a native Mongolian.

W. M. Ormrod, *The Reign of Edward III: Crown and Political Society in England, 1327–1377*. New Haven, CT: Yale University Press, 1990. A very detailed history that draws favorable conclusions about the abilities and perceptiveness of Edward.

W.M. Ormrod, ed., *England in the Fourteenth Century: Proceedings of the 1985 Harlowton Symposium*. Dover, NH: Boydell, 1986. This work includes Anthony Goodman's article "John of Gaunt," which concentrates on the character and political career of Edward III's controversial and influential son.

Otto of Freising, *The Deeds of Frederick Barbarossa*. Trans. Charles Christopher Mierow with the collaboration of Richard Emery. New York: W.W. Norton, 1966. A biography of Frederick Barbarossa written by his uncle.

Marcel Pacaut, *Frederick Barbarossa*. Trans. A.J. Pomerans. New York: Charles Scribner's Sons, 1970. Beginning with a history of the Holy Roman Empire as it existed in the twelfth century, this biography gives special attention to the situation and influence of Burgundy in the history of central Europe.

Régine Pernoud, *Blanche of Castile*. Trans. Henry Noel. New York: Coward, McCann & Geoghegan, 1975. A detailed biography of the mother of King Louis IX of France. It contains many cultural sidelights on life in France.

Régine Pernoud and Marie-Véronique Clin, *Joan of Arc: Her Story*. Trans. Jeremy Duquesnay Adams. Ed. Bonnie Wheeler. New York: St. Martin's, 1998. The best of French historical writing, which provides a clear picture of events while giving insight into the characters of Joan of Arc and King Charles VII of France.

Carla Rohr Phillips and William D. Phillips Jr., *Spain's Golden Fleece: Wool Production and the Wool Trade from the Middle Ages to the Nineteenth Century*. Baltimore: Johns Hopkins University Press, 1997. Provides background for a deeper understanding of the economic ties that bound Spain, England, and France.

Emma Pirani, *Gothic Illuminated Manuscripts*. New York: Hamlyn, 1970. Includes beautifully reproduced examples of illuminations from some prayer books of Louis IX and many others.

Fletcher Pratt, *The Battles That Changed History*. New York: Hanover House, 1956. Significant armed conflicts from the time of Alexander the Great to World War II.

Jonathan Riley-Smith, *The First Crusaders, 1095–1131*. Cambridge: Cambridge University Press, 1997. A study of the crusaders who defended Christendom in the Middle East.

John J. Robinson, *Dungeon, Fire, and Sword: The Knights Templar in the Crusades*. Provides insights into the life and character of crusaders.

Clifford J. Rogers, *War Cruel and Sharp: English Strategy Under Edward III, 1327–1360*. Woodbridge, UK: Boydell, 2000. This book makes a strong case that Edward III was a skillful strategist in the campaigns he led, both in his own country of England and overseas in parts of France.

Victoria Mary Sackville-West, *Saint Joan of Arc*. Literary Guild, 1936. A biography of Joan of Arc. Includes details of Joan of Arc's life that most other biographies miss.

Pamela Sargent, *Ruler of the Sky: A Novel of Genghis Khan*. New York: Crown, 1993. Sargent's fictional account, written from the point of view of the khan's many wives, builds skillfully on available information.

Tim Severin, *Tracking Marco Polo*. New York: Peter Bedrick, 1964. Severin and two companions rode motorcycles along the route taken by Marco Polo through the land of Genghis Khan.

R.A. Skelton, Thomas E. Marston, and George D. Painter, *The Vinland Map and the Tartar Relation*. New Haven, CT: Yale University Press, 1965. This work offers the complete text of a Franciscan friar's four-year trip to the land of Kublai Khan in 1245.

Mark Spencer, *Thomas Basin (1412–1490): The History of Charles VII and Louis XI*. Nieuwkoop, Netherlands: De Graaf, 1997. A detailed overview of the life and work of Thomas Basin, who was a contemporary biographer of Charles VII.

Jonathan Sumption, *The Albigensian Crusade*. London: Faber and Faber, 1978. Discusses the history, personalities, church politics, and mayhem in the time of Louis IX.

M.J. Swanton, trans. and ed., *The Anglo-Saxon Chronicle*. New York: Routledge, 1996. An early history of England.

Brian Tierney, Donald Kagan, and L. Pearce Williams, eds., *Gregory VII—Church Reformer or World Monarch?* New York: Random House, 1967. Provides primary source background concerning the religious struggles of William the Conqueror and Frederick Barbarossa.

Malcolm G.A. Vale, *Charles VII*. Berkeley and Los Angeles: University of California Press, 1974. An overview of the significance of Charles VII's reign and his country at the close of the Middle Ages.

W. Warburton, *Edward III*. New York: Charles Scribner's Sons, 1897. A biography that concentrates on historical relationships.

Periodicals

Antaeus, "Mustard: Not for Bread Alone," Spring 1992.

Michael Bennett, "Edward III's Entail and the Succession to the Crown," *English Historical Review*, June 1998.

James S. Bothwell, "'Escheat with Heir': Guardianship, Upward Mobility, and Political Reconciliation in the Reign of Edward III," *Canadian Journal of History*, August 2000.

Richard Cavendish, "The End of the Hundred Years' War, October 19th, 1453," *History Today*, October 2003.

Economist, "The Canonization of Genghis," February 10, 1990.

History Today, "End of the Hundred Years' War, October 19th, 1453," October 2003.

Elisabeth van Houts, "The Norman Conquest Through European Eyes," *English Historical Review*, September 1995.

Adam T. Kessler, "Genghis Khan: Treasures from Inner Mongolia," *USA Today*, May 1994.

Simon Lloyd, "The Crusades of St. Louis," *History Today*, May 1997.

D.A.L. Morgan, "The Political After-Life of Edward III: The Apotheosis of a Warmonger," *English Historical Review*, September 1997.

Thomas H. Oldgren, "Edwardus Redivivus in a Gest of Robyn Hode," *Journal of English and Germanic Philology*, January 2000.

W.M. Ormrod, "Edward III: The Career of the King," *History Today*, June 2002.

Willard Price, "Japan Faces Russia in Manchuria," *National Geographic*, November 1942.

Kenneth M. Setton. "900 Years Ago: The Norman Conquest," *National Geographic*, August 1966.

Anthony Verduyn, "The Politics of Law and Order During the Early Years of Edward III," *English Historical Review*, October 1993.

Childeric III (Frankish king), 9
China, 49–50
Christianity
    Charlemagne and, 10,
        15–16
    Charlemagne's father and, 9
    Genghis Khan and, 47
    Saxons and, 13
    William the Conqueror's
        rule and, 24
church, the. *See* Christianity
Conrad III (king of Germany),
    33–34
Costain, Thomas B., 28–30
Crécy, Battle of, 73–74
Crusades, the
    Frederick Barbarossa and,
        34, 40, 42
    Louis IX and, 58–61, 64–66

Damietta (Egypt), 58, 60–61
Desiderius (king of
    Lombardy), 9, 12
Domesday Book, 28–31

education
    Charlemagne and, 11–12
    under Genghis Khan, 53
Edward (king of England), 22
Edward the Confessor (king
    of England), 24–25
Edward III (king of England),
    7
    birth of, 69
    on conflict between nobility,
        70–71
    on crime, 77
    death of, 79
    deference to his mother,
        69–70

elected king, 69
France and, 73–77
last years of, 79
legacy of, 79
marriage of, 70
parents of, 69
on Scottish raiders, 70, 73
Spanish venture by, 77–79
England
    Charles VIII and, 82
    Louis IX's settlements with,
        63–64
    survey of land ownership in,
        28–31

Folz, Charles, 15, 16–17
France
    Edward III and, 73–77
    Queen Isabella and, 69
Franks
    alliance between the
        Lombards and, 9–10
    defeated by the Gascons,
        13
    winters among the, 10–12
Frederick Barbarossa (Holy
    Roman Emperor), 7
    birth of, 33
    death of, 42
    early fighting experience of,
        33–34
    as king of Germany, 34,
        35–36
    last military campaign of,
        40, 42
    legacy of, 42
    marriage of, 36–37
    military campaign in Italy
        by, 38–40
    parents of, 33

108

Lombard invasion of, 12

Sackville-West, Victoria Mary, 85
Salisbury oath, 28
Scottish raiders, 70, 73
Silk Road, 50–51
Sorel, Agnes, 87
Spain, 13, 63
St. Peter's Basilica (church), 16–17
suzerainty, 6

Tolui (son of Genghis Khan), 55
Tostig (Earl of Northumbria), 26
Toulouse University, 58
Treaty of Brétigny, 77
Treaty of Corbeil, 63
Treaty of Paris, 64
Treaty of Troyes, 82

troubadours, 19–20

Unggirat tribe, 43–44

William I. *See* William the Conqueror
William the Conqueror (king of England), 7
death of, 31
fighting by, 22–24
invasion of England by, 25–27
lands outside of England conquered by, 28
last days of, 31
legacy of, 31–32
loyalty to, 24
parents of, 21
prospects of ruling England by, 21–22, 24–25
rule over England by, 27–28
Wittekind (Widukind), 14

PICTURE CREDITS

ABOUT THE AUTHOR

Rafael Tilton reads, writes, and gardens in rural Montana, with a newly awakened interest in tracing her family history and genealogy, which may go all the way back to William the Conqueror.